北京市高等教育精品教材立项项目

英语时文泛读 (第4册)

Current News Articles for Extensive Reading

总主编　范守义
主　编　徐　英　魏腊梅

图书在版编目(CIP)数据

英语时文泛读(第4册)/范守义总主编. —北京:北京大学出版社,2009.6
(21世纪英语专业系列教材)
ISBN 978-7-301-14444-2

Ⅰ.英…　Ⅱ.范…　Ⅲ.英语－阅读教学－高等学校－教材　Ⅳ.H319.4

中国版本图书馆 CIP 数据核字(2009)第 171007 号

书　　　　名:	英语时文泛读(第 4 册)
著作责任者:	范守义　总主编
组 稿 编 辑:	张　冰
责 任 编 辑:	高生文
标 准 书 号:	ISBN 978-7-301-14444-2/H·2118
出 版 发 行:	北京大学出版社
地　　　　址:	北京市海淀区成府路 205 号　100871
网　　　　址:	http://www.pup.cn
电 子 邮 箱:	编辑部 pupwaiwen@pup.cn　　总编室 zpup@pup.cn
电　　　　话:	邮购部 62752015　发行部 62750672　编辑部 62755217　出版部 62754962
印 　刷 　者:	北京虎彩文化传播有限公司
经 　销 　者:	新华书店
	787 毫米×1092 毫米　16 开本　9.75 印张　200 千字
	2009 年 6 月第 1 版　2024 年 12 月第 6 次印刷
定　　　　价:	36.00 元

未经许可,不得以任何方式复制或抄袭本书之部分或全部内容。
版权所有,侵权必究
举报电话:(010)62752024　电子邮箱:fd@pup.cn

本书荣获
"李嘉诚学术基金"资助

写给本书使用者的话

21世纪的中国是改革向广度和深度进军的世纪，21世纪的世界是全球化走向优化整合和更高水平的世纪。中国与世界各国交往向全方位推进和巩固是历史发展之必然。走在历史发展最前沿的是双语或多语工作者；而在当今的世界上，英语使用之广泛是举世公认的。中国的外语教育中英语是最为重要的外国语言。外交学院作为外语类院校在过去的半个多世纪中为中国外交外事和各个部门培养了大批外语人才，他们在各个领域发挥了巨大作用，做出了杰出的贡献。

外交学院是具有外交特色和外语优势的重点大学，外交学院的英语教学在复校后的30年中，积累了丰富的教学经验。英语时文泛读是外交学院英语本科教学的核心课程；该课程为学生提高英语阅读水平，扩大词汇量和阅读技巧，丰富文化和国际知识提供了很好的学习平台。学习这门课程以及其他相关课程，可为学生走向职场奠定坚实的基础。外交学院培养出的学生具有国际视野和外交外事专业水准是十分恰当的评价。

2005年以来外交学院英语系将英语泛读作为精品项目立项，2007年夏被评为北京市精品课程；目前我们正在向国家级精品课程努力。该精品课程由两大板块组成，即课堂教学和课外阅读——课堂教学使用了精选的时文作为主要的教学内容；课外阅读使用了精选的英语简易读物、注释读物和英语原著作为主要内容，并为每一部书设计了100个问题，可以在计算机网络上进行在线测试，并立即得到结果，同时教师也能够立即看到全部参加测试者的成绩以及学生学期和学年的累计成绩。我们与北京外国语大学英语学院和首都师范大学外国语学院英语系合作，进行异地登录测试也取得了满意的结果。这种英语泛读课程创新的教学模式为迅速提高学生的英语水平和综合运用能力起到了很好的作用，深受教师和学生的欢迎。

这里我们主要谈一下课堂用书《英语时文泛读》的编写情况。

我们的编写设计思路如下：

1. 所选文本要语言地道、内容新颖（除个别为略早的文章，其余课文全部为2005年以后英美主要报刊杂志上发表的文章）、题材广泛多样（涉及政治、经济、文化、教育、科技、环保、法律、社会等诸方面内容），贴近时代与生活，易激发学生兴趣。

2. 该教材就不同主题设不同单元，知识内容较成体系，既有助于学生系统学习、积累和运用所学知识，又有助于学生分类学习记忆相关词汇。

3. 练习设计合理、实用，既有很强的针对性（针对每个单元具体的阅读技巧及目标），又能考察学生的综合能力，形式比较灵活，易于操作。

4. 为使所选用的文本难度符合学生的英语程度，既不要过易，也不要过难，我们根据美国著名教育家鲁道夫·弗莱什(Rudolf Flesch)博士的研究，即"英语文章难易度与单位长度的音节数和词数密切相关"的理论，将其数学模型化、程序化，并在其基础上进行《英语时文泛读》文本的选材，剔除了过难和过易的文本。

5. 编写了旨在为使用《英语时文泛读》的教师准备的《教师参考书》，提供必要而丰富的备课参考资料和练习答案。

6. 制作课堂使用的PPT文档，供授课使用，教师亦可增添或删节内容，以适应具体需要。

7. 编写快速阅读文本，以及相关的英国英语和美国英语的知识等内容，供教学参考使用。

8. 使用者可以根据本教学单位学生的英语水平，使用合适的单元和文本长度进行课堂阅读活动。

9. 为了锻炼学生自己查词典和确定词义的能力，在文本A和文本B之后的词汇表中，只给出没有在练习中出现的词；为照顾部分学生学习的需要，各单元的生词按英语字母顺序列在全书之后，学生可以查阅、记忆，然后再去做练习。

为保证教材编写的专业水准，我们组成了以范守义教授为负责人的《英语时文泛读》教程编写委员会，人员及任务分配如下：

范守义：总主编，负责策划统筹、审阅和编辑等工作。

石毅、于倩：共同主编，负责《英语时文泛读》第一册的编写工作；

张蕾、吴晓萍：共同主编，负责《英语时文泛读》第二册的编写工作；

武波、王振玲：共同主编，负责《英语时文泛读》第三册的编写工作；

徐英、魏腊梅：共同主编，负责《英语时文泛读》第四册的编写工作。

我们期待《英语时文泛读》的出版能够为我国大学本科和程度相当的英语学习者提供一套新的泛读教程，以满足与时俱进的教学要求；为此我们期待广大教师和学生提出宝贵意见和要求，以改进我们的编写工作。我们也期待以《英语时文泛读》为主和能进行在线测试的课外阅读为辅的创新英语泛读教学模式为推动和提升全国泛读教学做出贡献。

《英语时文泛读》教程编辑委员会

2008年12月26日

目录
CONTENTS

UNIT ONE   *FOOTBALL*   *1*

     Text A   Women's Football Popularity on the Rise / 1

     Text B   Officially Wrong / 7

     Text C   Ancient Chinese Football / 13

UNIT TWO   *ENTERTAINMENT*   *16*

     Text A   The Return of the Broadway Boogie-Woogie / 16

     Text B   Behold the Golden Age of Television / 22

     Text C   Your Own World / 30

UNIT THREE   *SEEING THE WORLD*   *35*

     Text A   Taking Our Time Off / 35

     Text B   Tourists Who Stay Close to Home / 41

     Text C   Capturing the Niche / 47

UNIT FOUR   *BUSINESS AND FINANCE*   *51*

     Text A   Land of the Giants / 51

     Text B   China on Credit / 57

     Text C   The Irish Question / 62

UNIT FIVE CHINA REPORT 68

Text A All Aboard / 68

Text B China 2.0 / 74

Text C China Juggles Tombs and Dragon Boats / 81

UNIT SIX CULTURAL DIFFERENCE 84

Text A China, U.S. Taking Notes on Education / 84

Text B Ambassador Bridge Controversy Highlights Cultural Divide / 91

Text C Love in a Cold and Wet Climate / 98

UNIT SEVEN ETHNICITY, GENDER AND GAY MARRIAGE 103

Text A I Won't Die for Equality / 103

Text B Blacks, Whites and Love / 108

Text C Oregon Supreme Court Invalidates Same-Sex Marriages / 114

UNIT EIGHT STRIVING FOR GOALS 118

Text A Let's Try Baloney / 118

Text B Thousands Rally for Immigrants' Rights / 124

Text C Tale of Two Presidents / 130

GLOSSARY / 134

UNIT ONE

FOOTBALL

Target of the Unit

☞ To get a glimpse of football game of men and women, the present and the past
☞ To practice reading skills
☞ To enlarge your vocabulary

1) LEAD IN

Directions: In this unit, you will read 3 passages about football as an international game, the predicament of women's football and its future, the men's football and some sordid dealings, and the Chinese origin of the game.

2) DISCUSSION

What does World Cup mean to our life? Will Chinese men's team emerge top 8, if not top 4 one day in the near future instead of disappointing us?

Text A

Women's Football Popularity on the Rise

By Jaskirt Dhaliwal

Warming-up Exercises

☞ When was it when the Chinese girls came into the limelight and won acclaim from the world's audience?
☞ Women of which country or countries are now the best football players?

1

First reading

Directions: Now please read the following passage as fast as you can and summarize the main idea.

1   It comes as little surprise that football has now replaced **netball** as the most popular female sport in England. When the FA took over the running of the women's and girls' game in 1993, there were just 11,200 registered players. Today that figure stands well over 100,000. Yet despite this rise, it still lags behind countries such as the United States where there are 7.8 million players.

2   For a country which claims **the beautiful game** as its heritage, why is it that the US women are more **revered** than our own?

netball n. Netball is a non-contact generally indoor sport similar to, and derived from, asketball. It is usually known as a women's sport. It was originally known in its country of origin, the United States, as "women's basketball". 是类似篮球的女子运动，最早的名字是叫"女子篮球"，起源于美国，创始人：Clara Gregory Baer，中文翻译有好几个，有"篮网球"，"投球"，"英式女篮"，没有统一的中文名字。风行於美、英、加、澳、纽及西印度群岛。即"无挡板篮球"或"女子篮球"。
rever v. to regard with awe, deference, and devotion 敬畏
sceptic n. someone who habitually doubts accepted beliefs 怀疑一切的人
propel v. to cause to move forward or onward 推动
limelight n. a focus of public attention 公众注意
plight n. a situation from which extrication is difficult especially an unpleasant or trying one 窘况

Sceptics or converts?

3   Under representation of women in sport, and football, is by no means an uncommon thing, you only have to look at the back pages of any newspaper to realise that, but after the success of Euro 2005, the times may be changing. Record attendances, impressive form, good TV ratings and an array of talent, all proved to **propel** the women's game into the **limelight** for a short time.

4   But now the competition is well and truly over, the new season has begun and any publicity gained has slowly fettered away. Only the dramatic **plight** of Birmingham City Ladies caught the public eye, after they were saved from imminent collapse and financial ruin in the 11th hour, proving miracles don't just happen in Instanbul!

Women's footy—good or bad?

5   However the effects are being felt, as Birmingham Ladies could no longer afford to hold

onto most of their top **acquisitions**, players like Rachel Yankey and Alex Scott, which had previously made them responsible for a quarter of England's Euro 2005 squad. But all is not doom and gloom. Having managed to keep starlets Karen Carney and recruit England keeper Jo Fletcher, the Blues are aiming to stay in the National Premier Division and build again.

6   Steve Shipway, Birmingham City Ladies FC's chairman since 2000, has seen the game grow rapidly since he first became involved with the club. "The women's game internationally has increased its profile with a lot more media coverage, a prime example being the **Euros** this year. But I've seen a much greater transformation at Blues. When I first started here there were only two teams, and now we have a centre of excellence and four full teams from under 10's and upwards, with the senior side competing in the highest women's football league."

7   Although the quality and quantity of players are undoubtedly rising, the spectators are unfortunately not. Steve commented, "Football has become the biggest female sport, ahead of netball, hockey ,etc., and the game will continue to grow. However where it isn't developing is as a spectator game. Even though we **(BCLFC)** play in the highest division we're still only getting an average attendance of 60-70 people every match. The lack of media coverage doesn't help."

8   Jenny Wilkes, Chairwoman of Wolverhampton Wanderers WFC, agreed. "The media coverage is a problem. It's a bit 'chicken and egg'—we need to get big gates to get the interest from the media, but we won't attract the crowds if the media don't cover the games. Wolves Women's average crowd is about 100-150—mainly friends and families of the players. It doesn't help that satellite TV is showing games all Sunday afternoon and the local newspaper doesn't publicise the games."

9   The progression of the women's game did see one team, Fulham, go professional for a season whilst under the financial wing of its male counterparts. But as soon as that financial backing was taken away,

> **acquisition** *n.* someone or something acquired or added 增添的人或物
> **Euro** *n.* Euro (Football) 200X 欧洲杯
> **BCLFC** *abbr.* Birmingham City Ladies Football Club 伯明翰市女足俱乐部

they slipped into **oblivion**.

10   This summer nearly saw the same with BCLFC, who were expecting financial help from the men's side, but astonishingly BCLFC's male counterparts couldn't afford £75,000 (an average players three month wages) to support the entire ladies team, because they believed it wasn't "commercially **viable**." Well neither is Emile Heskey, yet £6.25 million was still spent on him.

11   "I believe that one of the major problems in the game is the lack of support from the men's clubs. The most successful women's clubs, eg: Arsenal, Charlton, Everton have that support," said Jenny. "Many other clubs are really struggling to survive. Many of the men's clubs are only interested in profits and don't want to give anything back. I think the FA should MAKE the men's clubs take their female teams on board. They have made them run the girls' Centres of Excellence (for girls aged Under 10 to Under 16) but there are no requirements to help the senior teams."

> **oblivion** *n.* the condition or quality of being completely forgotten 彻底忘记
> **viable** *adj.* capable of success or continuing effectiveness; practicable 可行的
> **garner** *v.* to acquire or to deserve by one's efforts or actions 获得
> **euphoria** *n.* a feeling of great happiness or well-being 幸福感

12   If this is the case than by the time the World Cup comes around in 2007 how much progression will be made? "If the FA doesn't do something soon, it will be in exactly the same position as it is now—with many teams struggling to survive. The FA puts a lot of money and effort into the national side, but not into supporting the teams which provide the players for the squad. We don't want to see a repeat of England's poor performance at Euro 2005."

13   Jenny Wilkes' last comment rings very true, because although Euro 2005 gained lots of publicity for the women's game, it would have **garnered** a hell of a lot more if the England team had progressed into the latter stages of the tournament. It was their chance to spark national pride and **euphoria**, but instead they crumbled as is too often seen with the men's team. But with a fantastic grass roots development in place, hopefully England's ladies won't be too far off from reaching better heights next time round.

(Words: 918)

Second Reading

Directions: Read the text again more carefully to find enough information for Exercises I, II & III.

Exercise I True or False

Directions: Please state whether the following statements are true or false (T/F) according to what you've found in the text.

1. Football is as popular as netball for girls in England.
2. The beautiful game refers to football for girls.
3. Not much attention has been paid to women's football in England.
4. Because of the success in Euro 2005, women's football in England came into the limelight for a while.
5. People do not know the difficult situation Birmingham's girl's football team was in.
6. There are still chances for Birmingham Ladies to rise again.
7. Steve Shipway, Birmingham City Ladies FC's chairman is confident of women's football as an international game.
8. Women's football is a game that attracts large crowds of spectators.
9. Men's football clubs have given a great deal of help to their women counterparts.
10. Women's football did well at Euro 2005.

Exercise II Word Inference

Directions: Often you can guess the meaning of a word/expression by reading the words around it. Please read the given sentence to see how each word/expression in bold type is used in the text. Then choose the answer that is closest in meaning to the bold-faced word/expression.

1. When the FA took over the running of the women's and girls' game in 1993, there were just 11,200 **registered** players.
   A. on official list
   B. approved
   C. recognized
   D. publicized

2. Under **representation** of women in sport, and football, is by no means an uncommon thing, you only have to look at the back pages of any newspaper to realise that, but after the success of Euro 2005, the times may be changing.

   A. presence
   B. reproduction
   C. the state of being represented
   D. participation

3. Only the dramatic plight of Birmingham City Ladies caught the public eye, after they were saved from **imminent** collapse and financial ruin in the 11th hour, proving miracles don't just happen in Instanbul!

   A. belated
   B. impending
   C. urgent
   D. emergent

4. For a country which claims **the beautiful game** as its heritage, why is it that the US women are more revered than our own?

   A. women's football
   B. girl's football
   C. spectators game
   D. football

5. However the effects are being felt, as Birmingham Ladies could no longer afford to hold onto most of their top acquisitions, players like Rachel Yankey and Alex Scott, which had previously made them responsible for a quarter of England's Euro 2005 **squad**.

   A. scouts
   B. a small group
   C. a military unit
   D. an athletic team

6. The women's game internationally has increased its **profile** with a lot more media coverage, a prime example being the Euros this year.

   A. exposure to public notice
   B. status
   C. side view
   D. summery

7. The progression of the women's game did see one team, Fulham, go professional for a season whilst under the financial **wing** of its male counterparts.

   A. organization
   B. protection
   C. section
   D. support

8. It's a bit "**chicken and egg**"—we need to get big gates to get the interest from the media, but we won't attract the crowds if the media don't cover the games. This figure is used to liken the relationship between _____.

   A. stadium and media
   B. crowds and media
   C. games and media
   D. games and crowds

9. I think the FA should MAKE the men's clubs **take their female teams on board**.

   A. protect them
   B. be partners
   C. help them
   D. accept them

10. But with a fantastic **grass roots** development in place, hopefully England's ladies won't be too far off from reaching better heights next time round.
    A. the local level   B. basic
    C. unimportant   D. unofficial

Exercise III   Discussion
Directions: Please discuss the following questions in pairs or groups.

1. Do you agree that the Birmingham ladies' plight is typical of all other women's football teams?
2. What do you know about the present situation of China's women football teams?
3. What means more to the football fans, the World Cup, the European Cup or the Olympic Games?

Text B

Officially Wrong

By Bruce Crumley

Warming-up Exercises

☞ What do you think are the causes for referee errors and such scandals in sports?
☞ Is it a good idea to have referees from every continent of the world in sports? Will this guarantee impartiality?

• First reading •

Directions: Now please read the following passage as fast as you can and summarize the main idea.

1   ___A___. But while World Cup pressure seems to bring out some of the best field play, so far, this year at least, the officials have seemed noticeably incompetent. "They've been pretty bad," says an official with one of the squads favored to win it all—and who prefers not to make his team a target by identifying himself. "We haven't suffered the really terrible

decisions that others have. But we're probably the exception, not the rule."

2   To err is human, and by that score, the Cup's officiating crew have been made of all too solid flesh. The scary thing is, the referees actually appear to be getting worse. Back in 2002, repeated errors during the Cup's **knockout** round prodded FIFA officials to officially deny rumors that the **miscalls** were part of a plot to assist co-host South Korea advance towards the final. This time, conspiracy theorists began their **gripes** during the opening round. In the worse cases, bad decisions have altered scores, got players unjustly **expelled** or suspended, and showed the kind of consistency only a **schizophrenic** could love.

3   ____B____. In that same match, meanwhile, Ivanov refused to award France a penalty kick after Swiss defender Patrick Muller's hand irrefutably blocked striker Thierry Henry's shot from scoring. In their next game, Switzerland were similarly spared by Paraguayan referee Carlos Amarilla, who saw no ill in Muller's obvious foul as Togolese striker Emmanuel Adebayor charged toward the goal.

4   ____C____. Problem was, in all the excitement Michel forgot to slap Marquez the attendant yellow card—which spared the Mexican being sent off when he got booked in the second half. But the most glaring blunder of the Cup thus far came from veteran English ref Graham Poll, who flashed three yellow cards to defender Josip Simunicv of Croatia during their final match against Australia. Simunic was **booked** twice in the second half alone, but was amazingly allowed to play on—until he assailed Poll at the final whistle, and got the Englishman brandishing a third yellow card, followed by the belated red.

> **knockout** *n.* a competition in which competitors are eliminated progressively 淘汰赛
> **miscall** *v.* to call by a wrong name 点错名字,张冠李戴
> **gripe** *n.* sth unimportant that you complain about 抱怨,牢骚
> **expel** *v.* to officially force someone to leave a school or organization 驱逐,开除
> **schizophrenic** *n.* someone who has a serious mental illness in which his thoughts and feelings are not based on what is really happening around him 精神分裂症患者
> **book** *v.* (*sports*) to record the flagrant fouls of (a player) for possible disciplinary action, as in soccer 因犯规被记名

5   __D__. "Some of these guys aren't that bad, but have never officiated at this level, under this kind of pressure," the team official says—giving some Middle Eastern, South American and African refs as examples. "The ironic **upside** is, when refs have been bad, they're often bad both ways—both teams suffer."

6   __E__. In FIFA's effort to ensure each geographical region is fairly represented at the Cup, it encourages a balanced mix of referees—similar to its approach to teams from each zone. But that means officials who qualify aren't ultimately chosen as the best in the world, but the best possible from the various regions—where refereeing levels or philosophies may be better, worse or just a bit different than in others.

7   Indeed, geography seems unrelated to referee error in Cup play, as officials from virtually all regions have turned in performances ranging from commanding to borderline incompetent. Some say the deeper problem lies with officials simply having a harder time making the right calls in a sport that is getting faster by the day. Even professional refs admit the game moves so quickly—and now involves so many players using illicit efforts to gain advantage (principally by **faking fouls**)—that there is simply no way one man can get a good look at everything. Especially if he's rushing up and down a large **pitch** with players in front and behind him. Harried and at times bamboozled officials clearly need help—but how?

> **upside** *n.* an advantageous aspect 有利的方面
> **fake fouls** *v. phr.* pretend to foul 假犯规
> **pitch** *n.* A "football pitch" is the playing surface for the game of association football made of turf. Its dimensions and markings are defined by Law 1 of the Laws of the Game, "The Field of Play". 球场
> **pro** *n.* a professional, especially in sports 职业……

8   Gilles Veissiere, a French **pro** and international ref who retired last year, says officials will gladly accept assistance—but only certain kinds. Veissiere wouldn't object to seeing two central refs used—one for each end. "The majority of disputed calls take place in or near the penalty area, so assign a referee to cover each side of the pitch," Veissiere says. "Give football the same number of officials to cover fields of play that tennis and rugby do." Not a bad call. But not one that will right the wrongs suffered already by players and fans in the Cup—or prevent still more from sparking outrage before July 9.

(Words: 730)

• Second Reading •

Directions: Read the text again more carefully to find enough information for Exercises I, II, III & IV.

Exercise I Understanding Text Organization

Directions: You may find there are a few sentences (segments) missing from the passage. Read the article through and decide where the following sentences should go.

1. Are these normal human errors?
2. By contrast Slovakian ref Lubos Michel correctly granted Portugal a penalty last week after Mexican defender Rafael Marquez intentionally handled a ball that a rival player was poised to head home
3. Questioning the referee is nothing new: it's an **intrinsic** part of most organized sports, high or low
4. Part of the problem may be structural
5. Examples include Russian official Valentin Ivanov, who slapped France star Zinedine Zidane with a yellow card—his first in this Cup—for having taken a free kick before the whistle has sounded, normally considered a slight offense

Exercise II Multiple-choice Questions

Directions: Complete each of the following statements with the best choice given.

1. It seems referees' making unfair decisions is _____.
   A. the rule rather than the exception in the World Cup
   B. the exception rather than the rule in the World Cup
   C. not very commonplace in the World Cup
   D. suffered by all teams in the World Cup

2. Referee errors _____.
   A. are part of the conspiracy to assist co-host South Korea advance towards the final
   B. are getting worse now
   C. often alter scores
   D. are loved by schizophrenics

3. Examples of referee miscalls include _____.
   A. Ivanov awarding France a penalty kick
   B. Ivanov slapping Swiss defender Patrick Muller a yellow card
   C. Paraguayan referee Carlos Amarilla awarding Togolese striker Emmanuel Adebayor a yellow card
   D. Russian official Valentin Ivanov slapping Zinedine Zidane with a yellow card

4. The reasons that led to referee mistakes include all but _____.

   A. FIFA encourages a balanced mix of referees

   B. FIFA encourages teams from each zone

   C. officials chosen as referees aren't the best in the world

   D. refereeing philosophies vary in different parts of the world

5. One possible way to avoid referee mistakes is to _____.

   A. make the referees able to run as fast as the game goes

   B. provide referees with assistants

   C. put two central referees

   D. choose the most competent referees in the world

Exercise III   Word Inference

Directions: Often you can guess the meaning of a word/expression by reading the words around it. Please read the given sentence to see how each word/expression in bold type is used in the text. Then choose the answer that is closest in meaning to the bold-faced word/expression.

1. Questioning the referee is nothing new: it's an **intrinsic** part of most organized sports, high or low.

   A. internal   B. innate

   C. important   D. old

2. To **err** is human, and by that score, the Cup's officiating crew have been made of all too solid flesh.

   A. make mistakes   B. judge

   C. be angry   D. cheat

3. Back in 2002, repeated errors during the Cup's knockout round **prodded** FIFA officials to officially deny rumors that the miscalls were part of a plot to assist co-host South Korea advance towards the final.

   A. lead to   B. call on

   C. require   D. urge

4. In their next game, Switzerland were similarly spared by Paraguayan referee Carlos Amarilla, who saw no ill in Muller's obvious **foul** as Togolese striker Emmanuel Adebayor charged toward the goal.

   A. offense   B. violation of the rule

C. bad smell D. faking fall

5. But the most glaring **blunder** of the Cup thus far came from veteran English ref Graham Poll, who flashed three yellow cards to defender Josip Simunic of Croatia during their final match against Australia.
   A. severe punishment B. light punishment
   C. mistake D. scandal

6. Simunic was booked twice in the second half alone, but was amazingly allowed to play on—until he **assailed** Poll at the final whistle, and got the Englishman brandishing a third yellow card, followed by the belated red.
   A. attack B. swear at
   C. hurt D. overthrow

7. Simunic was booked twice in the second half alone, but was amazingly allowed to play on—until he assailed Poll at the final whistle, and got the Englishman **brandishing** a third yellow card, followed by the belated red.
   A. threaten B. wave
   C. command D. throw out

8. Even professional refs admit the game moves so quickly—and now involves so many players using **illicit** efforts to gain advantage (principally by faking fouls)—that there is simply no way one man can get a good look at everything.
   A. lots of B. flattering
   C. illegal D. honest

9. Harried and at times **bamboozled** officials clearly need help—but how?
   A. helpless B. angry
   C. incompetent D. confused

10. But not one that will right the wrongs suffered already by players and fans in the Cup—or prevent still more from sparking **outrage** before July 9.
    A. anger B. fighting
    C. wrongs D. peace

Exercise IV   Discussion

Directions: Please discuss the following questions in pairs or groups.

1. What can we do to prevent the scandals involving referees in sports?

2. Do you think referees alone are to be blamed for fake matches? Who is behind this?

3. What makes a country strong in sports?

Text C

Ancient Chinese Football

By Sevencastles

1   Centuries before football appeared in Europe, the Chinese had been practicing kicking balls with their feet to score points in organized matches. The ancient Chinese football, with similarities to today's football (soccer), is called "cuju" (literally "kick ball", as in Chinese "cu" means "kicking the ball with feet" and "ju" "a stuffed ball made of hide"). It originated in China, exported eastward to Japan and Korea, and westward to ancient Egypt, Greece, Rome, France and England. In 2004, FIFA, the governing body of football, claimed officially that Linzi (of China) was the birthplace of its game.

2   The games became popular during China's Warring States Period (476-221 BC), especially in Linzi (the capital of the Qi State, in today's Shandong Province in East China). Back then, it was used to train military cavaliers due to the fierce nature of the sport.

3   During the Han Dynasty (206 BC-AD 220), its popularity spread from the army to the royal courts and upper classes. It is said that even the Han emperor enjoyed the sport. At the same time, the games were standardized and rules established. Football matches were often held inside the imperial palace. A type of court was built especially for the matches, which had six crescent-shaped goal posts at each end. Since  the game could ward off leg numbness occurring after a long horseback ride, it also became a drill in army training. All prefectures had standard fields for training troops. Historical records say that during the war against the Huns, soldiers set up sports fields along the marching routes. This training lasted for many generations, and the game was always played during

troop inspections.

4   The sport was improved during the Tang Dynasty (618-907). The ball evolved from the previous feather-stuffed one into an air-filled one with a two-layered hull. Also, two different types of goal posts emerged: One was made by setting up posts with a net between them and the other consisted of just one goal post in the middle of the field. The then capital of Chang'an was filled with the football fields, in the backyards of large mansions, and some were even established in the grounds of the palaces. Soldiers who belonged to the imperial army and Gold Bird Guard often formed football teams for the delight of the emperor and his court. The level of female teams also improved. Records indicate that once a 17-year-old girl beat a team of army soldiers. The games even became popular amongst the scholars and intellectuals, and if a courtier lacked skill in the game, he could pardon himself by acting as a scorekeeper.

5   The sport flourished during the Song Dynasty (960-1279) due to social and economic development, extending its popularity to every class in society. In Water Margin (one of the four ancient Chinese masterpieces), the treacherous court official Gao Qiu was highly regarded by the emperor just because of his "cuju" skills. For instance, he could make the ball stick to his body. At that time, professional players were quite popular, and the sport began to take on a commercial edge. Professional players fell into two groups: one was trained by and performed for the royal court and the other consisted of civilians who made a living as players. The organizations were set up in large cities (now known as the earliest professional club) whose members were either lovers or professional performers. Non-professional players had to formally appoint a professional as his or her teacher and pay a fee before becoming a member. This process ensured an income for the professionals. Books on the game were also published. Historical finds such as copper mirrors or brush pots from the Song era often show scenes of professional performances. At that time, only one goal post was set up in the middle of the field.

6   But Chinese traditional ideas encouraged calm, peace and tolerance, so ancient sports in China were different from their more exciting and competitive versions in the West. The sport began its decline during the Ming Dynasty (1368-1644) due to neglect, and the 2,000-year-old

sport finally faded away.

7　　However, this ancient traditional Chinese-style soccer game was revived in September 2004, widely acknowledged as the origin of the modern football (soccer).

(Words: 703)

Exercise I Discussion

Directions: Please discuss the following questions in pairs or groups.

1. Please make an investigation into the rules of the early form of football in China?
2. What is the major difference between the early Chinese football and the modern international football in terms of the football pitch?
3. What was the Chinese philosophy regarding competitive games?

Exercise II Writing

Directions: Write a composition about your views on China's footballers, men and women, or about the making of a great athlete in about 200 words.

UNIT TWO

ENTERTAINMENT

Target of the Unit

☞ To get a glimpse of forms of entertainment in the American society
☞ To practice reading skills
☞ To enlarge your vocabulary

1) LEAD IN

Directions: In this unit, you will read 3 passages about various forms of entertainment in the American society. As you read them keep in mind what makes the American culture distinct from other cultures of the world.

2) DISCUSSION

What forms of entertainment young people like in today's Chinese society? Does it reflect any American influence?

Text A

The Return of the Broadway Boogie-Woogie

By Valerie Gladstone

Warming-up Exercises

☞ How do you like dancing performances? Do you know anything about the popular dance forms such as ballet, flamenco, tap-dance, folk dance, etc.?
☞ What forms of theatrical performance do you like best?

• First reading •

Directions: Now please read the following passage as fast as you can and summarize the main idea.

1   The choreographer Garth Fagan and Wynton Marsalis, the co-founder and artistic director of Jazz at Lincoln Center, go way back. They met in the 1980's when Mr. Fagan, a jazz aficionado, took his dancers to New York clubs to hear Mr. Marsalis play. "I knew we could learn from him," Mr. Fagan said in a recent conference call with Mr. Marsalis. "I sensed we saw things the same way." Eventually he invited Mr. Marsalis to a rehearsal at the company's headquarters in Rochester.

2   "I was young then—23 or 24," Mr. Marsalis said, "and for him to do a performance just for me, to show me that kind of respect, like I was Duke Ellington, was actually startling. I tried to understand the choreography as well as I could with my level of sophistication, which was very little at the time. But more than the choreography, I knew him. I could understand the genius of the man and his depth of understanding of world cultures, Afro and not Afro."

3   Mutual admiration led to collaboration. When the Brooklyn Academy of Music commissioned a full-evening work from Mr. Fagan for the Next Wave Festival in 1991, he asked Mr. Marsalis to compose the score. The result, "Griot New York," with dramatic sets by the sculptor Martin Puryear, is often cited as Mr. Fagan's finest achievement.

4   But because of scheduling difficulties, the work, which vividly captures the city's vitality and diversity as well as its chilling indifference to the disenfranchised, has not been performed in New York in its entirety since its premiere. On Wednesday, however, Garth Fagan Dance, accompanied by Mr. Marsalis on trumpet with his septet, will perform the piece at Jazz at Lincoln Center. On other programs during the **troupe's** engagement through Nov. 13, are the premiere of "Life: Dark/Light" set to a score by the jazz violinist Billy Bang, excerpts from "Griot New York" and other works from the **repertory**.

5   Mr. Fagan, 65, who choreographed

> **troupe** n. a group of singers, actors, dancers, etc. who work together 剧团
> **repertory** n. a type of theatre work in which actors perform different plays on different days 不同时间的演出剧目

the Broadway hit "The Lion King," and Mr. Marsalis, 44, warmly recalled their collaboration on "Griot New York," which began with Mr. Fagan sending Mr. Marsalis a poem he had written with the same title, sketching out some of his themes. Like a West African griot, a storyteller who preserves traditions and culture, Mr. Fagan's work touches on what he saw as New York's most striking qualities, joyful and sad. He included references to African countries, and places with beautiful names like Bujumbura, and dealt with slavery and AIDS. "Being the artist he is," Mr. Fagan said, "I knew he could grasp what I was trying to do."

6   There had never been any question that Mr. Fagan would choose jazz for "Griot New York." "Jazz is America's music," he said. "It has all the structure of classical music and all the freedoms and passions of America. We do real jazz dancing to this man's score. We become like sidemen, dancing in and out of the music."

7   Already trained in a vigorous, highly rhythmic style—a fusion of African, Caribbean and modern dance and ballet techniques—Mr. Fagan's dancers find in "Griot New York," with many sequences set to **calypso**, blues and other social dance forms, an occasion to display their extraordinary virtuosity and musicality.

8   Mr. Marsalis said that he felt completely at ease composing for dance. "Our music is dance," he said of jazz. "A lot of our big grooves are called dance grooves. It's much better for us when it's with dance. Garth brings a new consciousness to us. We see his work and say, 'Man, look at this **counterpoint** and these different things he has in his dances, dancers dancing in different times, using their bodies in different ways.' The stuff is so inspiring to us."

9   With Mr. Fagan's themes in mind, Mr. Marsalis wrote a score with sudden and abrupt contrasts similar to what he admires in certain paintings. "The form that I often used is collage," he said. "It cuts from one thing to another, like New York from one block to another, like Stuart Davis's paintings. Or a certain type of Romare Bearden collage: it has the feeling of the city, but it also deals with country themes. It's cutting back and forth with a lot of swift, angular things. New York is the sound of counterpoint. There is a lot going on in the city, all organized by form and space—that's a jazz concept because we use space to organize whatever we play."

> **Calypso** *n.* a type of Caribbean song based on subjects of interest in the news 卡利普所，一种加勒比音乐形式，以当前新闻中关注话题为主题的歌曲
>
> **counterpoint** *n.* The technique of combining two or more melodic lines in such away that they establish a harmonic relationship while retaining their linear individuality [音乐]对位

10 They worked on the piece for several months, separately and with the dancers, often conferring by phone. Mr. Fagan, who was born in Jamaica, choreographed the dance in eight

sections, hoping to convey the varied experiences of New Yorkers, especially of Africans and of blacks from the Caribbean. When something didn't quite **mesh**, they adapted.

11   "Wynton came to us with the music for the love duet 'Spring Yaoundé,'" Mr. Fagan said, "but when he saw it, he said, 'No, man, I'm not going to use this,' and he tossed away what he'd come with, and sat down at the piano, and with one hand on the keys, he put his trumpet to his mouth and just composed an extraordinary ballad right there. I mean the damn walls were crying with emotion by the end of it."

12   In **ravishingly** sensual duets like "Spring Yaoundé," in which the dancers wind themselves around each other and end with their faces so close they appear as one, Mr. Fagan shows varieties of romantic love—interracial, gay and straight. "People need someone they can count on," Mr. Fagan said. "That is the essence of mankind, working and making love and growing and supporting each other."

> **mesh** v. to fit together closely or work in harmony 配合密切，工作协调
> **ravishingly** adv. extremely attractive; entrancing 十分迷人地，令人倾倒地
> **interlude** n. a short piece of music, talk, etc. used to fill a short period of time between the parts of a play, concert, etc. 间奏曲
> **pit** n. an orchestra pit 乐池

13   Mr. Fagan thought it was important to have an **interlude** with Mr. Marsalis and his septet alone onstage to simulate a jazz concert in a club. For all the other sections, they play in the **pit**. But jazzmen like to play something different every night, so he had to beg them to play the same notes at every performance.

14   "Sometimes Garth told us we were making too much noise down there," Mr. Marsalis said, recalling the good times his septet and Mr. Fagan's dancers spent together on tour with the piece in 1993. "We'd be making stuff up and acting crazy, changing parts, clowning around. We're kind of mischievous that way. At least we were like that then."

15   Even though 14 years have passed since Mr. Fagan choreographed "Griot New York," he doesn't think the work has become dated. "All the same elements in the city are still there, in more and lesser degrees," he said.

16   Will they work together again? "Absolutely," Mr. Fagan said. "The next piece I do with Wynton will be a collaboration to be premiered at his new theater. Within the next two years."

17   Not missing a beat, Mr. Marsalis said, "I'm going to hold him to that."

(Words 1185)

Second Reading

Directions: Read the text again more carefully to find enough information for Exercises I, II & III.

Exercise I   True or False

Directions: Please state whether the following statements are true or false (T/F) according to what you've found in the text.

1. Mr. Fagan and Mr. Marsalis first met in Lincoln Center, Rochester.
2. Mr. Fagan specially put up a show for Mr. Marsalis because there exist great chances for the two to cooperate.
3. In 1991, Mr. Fagan and Mr. Marsalis designed the dance moves of "Griot New York."
4. Wednesday will be the first time "Griot New York" shown in its full length in New York City.
5. "Griot New York" deals with themes such as life in African countries.
6. The choreography of "Griot New York" is a fusion of African, Caribbean and modern dance and ballet techniques.
7. A lot of famous Jazz albums are called dance albums because jazz music is very suitable for dancing.
8. In certain paintings of "Griot New York" we can find a lot of sudden and abrupt contrasts.
9. "Griot New York" depicts the life of blacks, especially those from the Caribbean, in New York.
10. The choreography of "Spring Yaoundé" is so designed as to show the varieties of romantic love.

Exercise II   Word Inference

Directions: Often you can guess the meaning of a word/expression by reading the words around it. Please read the given sentence to see how each word/expression in bold type is used in the text. Then choose the answer that is closest in meaning to the bold-faced word/expression.

1. They met in the 1980's when Mr. Fagan, a jazz **aficionado**, took his dancers to New York clubs to hear Mr. Marsalis play.
   A. expert
   B. professional
   C. enthusiast
   D. director

2. I tried to understand the **choreography** as well as I could with my level of sophistication, which was very little at the time.
   A. arrangement of steps
   B. dancers
   C. music
   D. formation

3. I tried to understand the choreography as well as I could with my level of **sophistication**, which was very little at the time.
   A. wisdom
   B. knowledge
   C. experience
   D. delicacy

4. But because of scheduling difficulties, the work, which vividly captures the city's **vitality** and diversity as well as its chilling indifference to the disenfranchised, has not been performed in New York in its entirety since its premiere.
   A. important things
   B. business
   C. liveliness and vigor
   D. crowdedness

5. But because of scheduling difficulties, the work, which vividly captures the city's vitality and diversity as well as its chilling indifference to the **disenfranchised**, has not been performed in New York in its entirety since its premiere.
   A. ethnic minority
   B. underprivileged
   C. uneducated
   D. handicapped

6. On Wednesday, however, Garth Fagan Dance, accompanied by Mr. Marsalis on trumpet with his **septet**, will perform the piece at Jazz at Lincoln Center.
   A. instrument
   B. group of seven
   C. group of nine
   D. players

7. There had never been any question that Mr. Fagan would choose jazz for "**Griot** New York."
   A. slave
   B. musician
   C. dancer
   D. story teller

8. Mr. Fagan's dancers find in "Griot New York," with many sequences set to calypso, blues and other social dance forms, an occasion to display their extraordinary **virtuosity** and musicality.
   A. excellent skill
   B. virtues
   C. sense of rhythm
   D. figures

9. "The form that I often used is **collage**," he said.
   A. putting scenes together   B. contrasting
   C. confusion   D. cutting back and forth
10. "The next piece I do with Wynton will be a collaboration to be **premiered** at his new theater. Within the next two years."
   A. shown   B. shown for the first time
   C. composed   D. rehearsed

Exercise III Discussion
Directions: Please discuss the following questions in pairs or groups.

1. Do you like the Broadway hit "The Lion King," choreographed by Mr. Fagan? Why or why not?
2. The extravagance of the Olympic opening ceremony and the closing ceremony choreographed by Zhang Yimo has impressed the world. Do you think the results would have been better if Steven Spielberg had agreed to come to help?

Text B

Behold the Golden Age of Television
By Tony Hall

Warming-up Exercises

☞ What are the functions TV broadcast has served to the community?
☞ Do you like to watch TV and does watching TV do you some good? Or harm?

First reading

Directions: Now please read the following passage as fast as you can and summarize the main idea.

1   There's a myth that older TV people—particularly those who have stepped out of the business—like to promote. TV isn't what it was, they say. We have just passed through a golden age, and now we are heading for cultural darkness.

2   Since leaving the BBC, I have been able to watch television **in a different light**. Indeed, as a viewer I think I now see it more clearly than I ever did. It is much easier to appreciate its strengths, and understand its weaknesses too.

3   What I like about British television is its quality and range. Of course not everything excites me, but there is plenty to be optimistic about, especially in terms of arts coverage.

4   The BBC series *A Picture of Britain* this summer showed that it is possible to put a thoughtful, thought-provoking, well-researched arts programme right in the middle of primetime viewing on Sunday evenings. It was popular, intelligent and engaging, it linked to a book and an exhibition at the Tate, and it was exactly what public service broadcasters such as the BBC and Channel 4 should be—and are—doing to reflect the arts in Britain.

> **in a different light** *prep. phr.* If someone or something is seen or shown in a particular light, people can see that particular part of their character 刮目相看
> **jerky** *adj.* foolish, silly 傻里傻气的

5   So it seems to me that far from leaving behind the golden age of television, we are still living through it. But we have reached a stage where, very soon, television will never be the same again. Broadcasting is about to discover democracy. Increasingly it will be the consumers who dictate what appears on screen. Far from narrowing the choice of programming, I believe this can broaden and enrich it.

6   Think back to the London bomb attacks in early July. What made the coverage so compelling were the informal ways of gathering information: emails, texts, pictures and snips of video from mobile phones. The half-lit images of the smoke-filled tunnels were unforgettable. The story unfolded not through the polished phrases of traditional broadcasters, but through the eyes of ordinary people caught up in the horror.

7   But this revolution will change far more than news. The balance of power between the broadcasters and the audience is shifting, brought about by the new ways we can both record and receive information. You can see it reflected in those **jerky** images on the news, but you can also sense it when you look at the iPod. Right now it is for listening, but before long something very similar will also be a means of viewing. Then the power of the consumer to choose what, when and where they watch could blow apart everything we are used to. When we all own television iPods, we will also be able to dictate where we watch, and demand the ability to download both current and archived material to suit the mood of the moment.

8   For me this vision of the future centres on the train I take to work. I have a long commute, and I can't wait to use it to watch the programmes I missed last night. I already  **cherry-pick** programmes to hear on the BBC radio player via the website. When the BBC applies the same logic to television—and it is already being planned—it will be truly extraordinary. For people like me who don't have a huge amount of time and who really want to watch television, but have so far been limited because we can rarely catch the programmes we like, it means a complete change in our viewing habits.

9   This does not imply a breakdown of all formality. There will still be news bulletins presented by newscasters and specialist reporters, there will still be schedules. But at the same time a breeze will blow into dusty corners. It will be interesting to see how television channels and broadcasters exploit these opportunities, but this is also a chance for organisations outside broadcasting to start thinking in new ways, including promoters of the arts such as the Royal Opera House.

_____A_____.

10   Arts coverage on TV has undoubtedly improved in recent years but nothing beats the excitement of watching a live performance in a theatre, opera house or concert hall. However, relatively few people can do that. The next best thing is to have a performance on screen, wherever and whenever you choose to watch it. Through broadband we have a chance to give people access live to what happens on stage at the opera house, or to offer them the secondary experience of downloading a performance after the event.

11   We are not setting out to launch The Opera House Channel, but I do believe there is a real opportunity here for arts organisations. Broadcasting will become like a vast bookshop into which the viewer wanders, saying to him or herself: right now, this is what I want to watch.

> **cherry-pick** v. to choose the best things or people you ant from a group before anyone else has the chance to take them 抢先挑选

12   It could be the same for sport. You may not want to watch the live broadcast of the Brazilian Grand Prix or the England versus New Zealand rugby test match because in your time zone it is the middle of the night. Instead you download and watch it the next day. This makes for an enormous expansion of cultural richness.

13   My instinct is that this is the way of the future. So we have cut a deal with Sony and installed high definition cameras at the opera house. There are rights issues to be sorted, and copyright. But against the negatives, we can balance the overwhelming benefit of expanding our audience for the arts to a global audience.

14   In Britain we are exceptionally well placed. Few other places can match the range of our theatres, galleries, museums and concert halls. My worry is whether broadcasters are still prepared to put in the money and time to exploit this richness. But I am cheered by the fact that television this year has been prepared to make big statements, and big commitments, like the superb Live8 concerts, or Channel 4's commitment to looking at torture and human rights. Creatively, British television remains in a good place.

B

15   It is not enough to make it possible for an audience to watch in the way I describe. You have to make sure the right people are part of the conversation that tells them what is happening, so they know when to watch or what to download. Marketing is essential, and one reason for working with broadcasters, rather than setting up our own channel, is to have access to the broadcaster's marketing machinery. Being seen or heard on big audience channels leads people to you. But the balance may change.

16   Consumers of the arts are much the same as shoppers. You can use a boutique or you can use a department store—it is essentially the brands that bring people to the product. We sell ourselves over the web, and I was amazed by how many more potential customers we can identify in this way: 70 per cent of the people who visit our website are new to the opera house. Moreover, the relationship that can be opened up with an audience through email is an unusually personal and **proactive** one. We have been asking students how they use the opera house, and they tell us they want emails, to be reminded that something is happening or to hear about special deals.

> **proactive** *adj.* making things happen or change rather than reacting to events 积极主动的

17   Developments like these suggest that marketing the arts—and by extension the broadcasting of the arts—will become much more finely targeted. Once we discover that someone is a particular fan of Rossini, for example, we can tell from our database whether

they have booked for the Rossini opera to be staged in a few months' time. Then we email them to remind them about it.

18   Text messaging is just as powerful. You can send a message alerting those on your database to a performance you think they will like, or promoting one where ticket sales have been slow, or telling them a performance can be downloaded to their TV iPod.

19   It is easy **to be dismissive of** some of the programming that the new forms of television distribution offer us. There are moments when I am tempted to assume a lofty position and **sneer** that topless darts or non-stop poker is not what I went into television for. But the fact that **niche** channels survive also suggests that the multi-channel environment can offer broadcasting of real cultural worth; look at some of the big ideas Channel 4 is proposing for More4.

_____C_____.

20   Niche audiences are often free with their criticism or praise, and they are even quicker to give feedback when they have an interactive red button to hand. If most of this is telling you how much your humble efforts are appreciated, it will be tempting to go on doing what you do so well to please the audience. The danger is that broadcasters will stick to what they know the audience responds positively to. But we have to dare to be innovative, even at the risk of failure; risk is essential to creativity. In today's climate, when wasting programme budgets or public funds is one of the seven deadly sins, it is not always easy. You have to address the idea that you will, at some point, fail, and see that as a positive.

_____D_____.

21   Despite my optimism, perhaps it is only right to end on a note of caution. As we all become more discriminating, more specialised in what we watch, choosing niche channels, the question becomes: what will bring us together? One thing that makes this country special is our diversity. But the more divided we become in the way we use media, the job of communicating the common ground between us becomes much, much harder. One of the terrifying things to come out of the London bombings, and the debate about Iraq, is the level of misunderstanding about and between the communities that make up Britain.

22   The big journalistic or editorial

---

to be dismissive of *phr.* refusing to consider someone or something seriously 不屑一顾
sneer *v.* to smile or speak in a very unkind way that shows you have no respect for someone or something 讥讽
niche *n.* an opportunity to sell a product or service to a particular group of people who have similar needs, interests, etc. 针对具有类似需求或兴趣的产品或服务

question that broadcasters have to face in the next five to 10 years is how to reflect this variety of cultures. How do we avoid **stereotypes**, caricature or cultural ghettos? What is the balance between free speech and divisive polemic? What restrictions will broadcasters, and artists, have to suffer to maintain proper relationships between those communities? In Birmingham, a play was taken off because of protest from one section of the community that found it offensive.

> **stereotype** *n.* a belief or idea of what a particular type of person or thing is like, often unfair or untrue 成见
> **behold** *v.* to see or look at sth 看呀

23　　Back in that mythical golden age, television was the great cultural unifier in Britain. In some senses it still is: I find it fascinating that *Big Brother* draws strong nationwide audiences by showing us a group of people who sometimes get along, but more often don't. Can television still somehow bring us together in the multi-channel future? This time the answer will have to come not from the broadcasters, but the consumers.

(Words: 1434)

· Second Reading ·

Directions: Read the text again more carefully to find enough information for Exercises I, II, III & IV.

Exercise I Understanding Text Organization

Directions: You may find there are a few sentences (segments) missing from the passage. Read the article through and decide where the following sentences should go.

1. Taking risks
2. Targeting television and the arts
3. Reaching out
4. Television and the arts

Exercise II Multiple-Choice Questions

Directions: Please choose the best answer to the following questions.

1. The author thought that the golden age of TV _____.
   A. had been over and now it is cultural darkness

B. was still in process

C. will happen in the near future

D. will soon be replaced by a future where television will never be the same again

2. What is not the change happening to TV?

   A. Ordinary people are contributing first-hand images or accounts to some big news.

   B. The audience could decide what, when and where to watch.

   C. News bulletins will be broadcast by ordinary people rather than the traditional newscasters.

   D. People can use their television iPod to download and watch the programmes they like.

3. What are the possible problems of broadcasting opera house shows through Sony high definition digital camera?

   A. People prefer sitting in theaters for the shows to watching on TV.

   B. The overwhelming high cost of expanding to a global audience of arts.

   C. The unreliable technique.

   D. Rights issues and copyright.

4. What is not the way suggested by the author for arts to reach the audience?

   A. Do promotion in boutiques and department stores where there are a lot of people.

   B. Broadcaster's marketing machinery.

   C. Email.

   D. Text message.

5. The author thinks that failure in the broadcaster's work is _____.

   A. avoidable because broadcasters always appeal to the audience's tastes

   B. a positive thing, because risk is essential to creativity

   C. one of the seven deadly sins, for the budget or funds wasted

   D. indicative of the lack of creativity

Exercise III Word Inference

Directions: Often you can guess the meaning of a word/expression by reading the words around it. Please read the given sentence to see how each word/expression in bold type is used in the text. Then choose the answer that is closest in meaning to the bold-faced word/expression.

1. There's a **myth** that older TV people—particularly those who have stepped out of the business—like to promote.
   A. tradition
   B. habit
   C. age-old story
   D. possibility

2. There's a myth that older TV people—particularly those who have stepped out of the business—like to **promote**.
   A. publicize
   B. complain
   C. feel nostalgic
   D. tell

3. What I like about British television is its quality and range. Of course not everything excites me, but there is plenty to be **optimistic** about, especially in terms of arts coverage.
   A. confident
   B. excited
   C. critical
   D. happy

4. The BBC series *A Picture of Britain* this summer showed that it is possible to put a thoughtful, thought-provoking, well-researched arts programme right in the middle of **primetime** viewing on Sunday evenings.
   A. early in the evening
   B. late in the evening
   C. the time with the most viewers
   D. most important time

5. Broadcasting is about to discover democracy. Increasingly it will be the consumers who **dictate** what appears on screen.
   A. produce
   B. decide
   C. pay for
   D. attack

6. What made the coverage so **compelling** were the informal ways of gathering information: emails, texts, pictures and snips of video from mobile phones.
   A. extremely exciting and interesting
   B. moving
   C. unprofessional
   D. unattractive

7. When we all own television iPods, we will also be able to dictate where we watch, and demand the ability to download both current and **archived** material to suit the mood of the moment.
   A. future
   B. past
   C. filed
   D. up-to-date

8. But I am cheered by the fact that television this year has been prepared to make big statements, and big **commitments**, like the superb Live8 concerts, or Channel 4's commitment to looking at torture and human rights.
   A. progress
   B. achievements

C. preparations	D. pledge

9. But we have to dare to be *innovative*, even at the risk of failure; risk is essential to creativity.

   A. risky	B. able to bring about new things, changes, etc.
   C. humble	D. moderate

10. How do we avoid stereotypes, caricature or cultural ghettos? What is the balance between free speech and divisive *polemic*?

    A. dialogue	B. publication
    C. activity	D. forceful speech

Exercise IV Discussion

Directions: Please discuss the following questions in pairs or groups.

1. What are the possible problems which will arise out the future way of people using the media?
2. Do you agree with the author on his view of the relationship between the audience and the broadcasters? What's you view?

Text C

Your Own World

By Rana Foroohar

1   The world's largest broadcaster first glimpsed the future of entertainment through the eyes of grade-school kids and grannies. Jana Bennett, director of television for the British Broadcasting Corp., remembers the shock well. The BBC was trying to get a grip on how new technologies are changing the way people use television, radio and new media. So in April 2004 the top brass invited "extreme users," those most deeply engaged in multimedia and Web sites, to chat. Expecting stereotypical geeks, they instead met grade-schoolers broadcasting their own music mixes created from BBC's radio Web pages, homemakers publishing online, and a "Gaming Granny" deep into multiplayer fantasy games. "We were blown away," remembers Bennett. "We realized there were large numbers of people out there doing things

that we weren't doing."

2   That realization lit a fire under the BBC, and this fall, the venerable company will begin rolling out its new digital self. For starters, more than 50 percent of the fall television lineup will be available for free download over the Internet, as the broadcaster tests a new digital video-on-demand system. Meanwhile, the BBC will also be delivering snippets of top comedy shows to mobile phones, in a trial run for a TV-to-phone service, with more to come. All BBC producers are now required to think about how each new project might play out over every kind of medium and device. "Entertainment is no longer linear," says Bennett. "You have to think in terms of a broader life cycle of a show—how it will play on TV or computer, in a game, on a phone—and you have to embrace a new kind of creative partnership with your audience."

3   The BBC's new strategy reflects two important truths of 21st-century media. Just as all politics is local, all news and entertainment is now personal—in the digital age, users can manipulate media to do what they want. Thanks to high-speed broadband pipes and peer-to-peer technology that puts more computing power in the hands of individuals, it's become much easier to create and manipulate media online. In this new world, consumers, as much as creators, are in control.

4   Secondly, the Internet changes the timeline of entertainment production, broadcast and consumption. Instead of a movie opening on the big screen, then trickling down to television, video and the Internet, it can appear in all formats at once, as 2929 Entertainment plans to do with new Steven Soderbergh releases. At the same time, in a world of digital choice, people can ignore your offerings, but they can also keep watching, reading or listening forever. That concept, famously dubbed the "Long Tail" by *Wired* editor Chris Anderson, also changes the entire economic model of entertainment, creating hugely successful **niche** products over longer periods of time.

5   That doesn't mean that the blockbuster movie, album, or TV series goes away. In many ways, it gets more important, as media companies put bigger bucks into marketing top products over multiple devices, and consumers look for standouts in a crowded lineup. "Event entertainment is getting bigger," says Bennett, citing the recent BBC nature series "Coast," which attracted 5 million viewers, or 21 percent of the viewing population. "That's a lot more than we would have gotten five years ago."

6   That fact belies fears that the new world of entertainment will be isolating. It's true that digital media allows for endless personalization: Mom and Dad can watch separate TV shows, while Sister trades photos with online friends and so on. But the Internet also creates new opportunities for connection. Blogs and photo-sharing Web sites are thriving, and new

communities of online DJs and filmmakers are springing up. Viewers are trading the made-for-mobile-phone dramas called mobisodes, or building virtual communities around Web broadcasts (many viewers of "Coast" used the BBC Web site to organize real-life coastal walks around Britain). The BBC is currently working on a digital storytelling project that would encourage kids to make their own documentaries online. "A lot of great television has been made by the public," Bennett says.

7   That includes the news. During recent events like the Southeast Asian tsunami and Hurricane Katrina, major networks rebroadcast pictures and reports from on-scene bloggers. In an April speech, Rupert Murdoch said that News Corp. might "experiment with the concept of using bloggers to supplement our daily coverage of news on the Net." Of course, there are some big questions about how you control quality among citizen bloggers, but solutions are already emerging. Take Wikipedia.org, the online, user-generated encyclopedia. Anyone can edit a page, which could theoretically lead to total anarchy. Instead, the community of users are themselves so involved and diligent that spam or misinformation tends to come down as quickly as it goes up. Wikipedia is a nonprofit, but some venture capitalists say that the advertising potential of the site could make it a billion-dollar business (community members have thus far bucked any movement in that direction).

8   So where does all this leave the traditional news and entertainment companies? Plenty (especially in Hollywood) are fearful of being put out of business by Google and Yahoo as they move forward with their efforts to control the "bundle" of voice, data and video search technology, and Yahoo, under the leadership of former Warner Brothers chairman and CEO Terry Semel, is moving more and more of its staff from Silicon Valley to L.A. As the worlds of media, technology and telecommunications collide, there will undoubtedly be more and more interesting new pairings (witness eBay's rumored bid for Internet phone provider Skype). The major dot-coms have massive market capitalizations, as well as the all-important search technology and huge, and hugely revealing, customer databases. (Hollywood still can't figure out who the audience for any given movie is.)

9   As 21st-century entertainment arrives, content will remain crucial. Its owners may not. Veteran entertainment investment banker Herb Allen says that as the Internet continues to cut

out the middleman, it is the individual entertainment properties, rather than their corporate wrappers, that will increase in value. "Do videogames, top sports leagues and Discovery documentaries have a future? Absolutely. Do department-store style networks? I'm not so sure."

10   While the gatekeepers may be in danger, producers and editors will become more important. Choice paralysis is a fact—studies have shown that people become overwhelmed and shut down when offered as few as 12 different options—Nielsen data show that even people who receive hundreds of channels tune in on only a dozen or so of them regularly. Virtual editors will play a growing role in the form of more sophisticated search engines that can scan not only text, but music and video, locating your favorite action scene in an old movie or a particular joke from a 1950s sitcom.

11   There are those, even within the tech world, who worry about these automated editors. We are fast moving toward a world in which engineers and algorithms have as much effect on content selection as creative media types. "What happens to something—a story, a play, a research paper or an event—if Google decides, for whatever reason, that it's not important?" asks European venture capitalist Danny Rimer, one of the investors in Skype. Perhaps it will disappear altogether. Or perhaps it will simply make its way down the Long Tail of the Internet to the one-in-a-million consumer who will truly appreciate it.

12   Whatever the answer, technology is already changing the process of media production, broadcast and consumption in countless ways. Producers are experimenting with multiple story lines that allow viewers to select their own endings. Computerized special effects are further blurring the lines between movies and videogames. Commercials are becoming interactive stories. While there will be casualties in this chaos, it's unlikely that any form of entertainment will die out completely. "When TV came along, radio became audio wallpaper, and movies, which had been the ubiquitous media, became the special event," notes futurist Paul Saffo. Even as DVDs have put cinematic revenues into free fall, theaters are already reinventing themselves as destination attractions with gourmet menus and child care.

13   As the BBC rolls out its fall lineup, Jana Bennett has asked other division heads to participate in a time-capsule exercise, placing their bets for the future of digital entertainment. "Nobody could have predicted the mobile revolution 10 years ago," she says. "I think it will be interesting in a few years to see how wrong we all are about this." Whatever they are watching, on whichever device, it's safe to say that the consumers of tomorrow's entertainment will be doing their own thing.

(Words 1435)

Exercise I Discussion

Directions: Please discuss the following questions in pairs or groups.

1. How is the new trend of entertainment described in the text affecting your life? Can you give daily examples to prove your points?
2. What do you think of the involvement of individuals in entertainment? Will this lead to anarchy, or democracy in media?
3. How do you predict the future of entertainment and media?

Exercise II Writing

Directions: The articles in this unit are related to entertainment. Write a composition about the form of entertainment that has brought you the greatest pleasure in about 200 words.

UNIT THREE

SEEING THE WORLD

Target of the Unit

☞ To learn about what the growth of tourism industry has brought about to people's life style and their tastes
☞ To practice reading skills
☞ To enlarge your vocabulary

1) LEAD IN

Directions: In this unit, you will read 3 passages about people's preference for taking leisurely, in-depth holidays, spending money on buying luxurious articles, or personalized tour to satisfy special needs. As you read think about what tourism industry can do in terms of adding to the GDP of a country.

2) DISCUSSION

Do you prefer to travel by rail, road, air or water? Why?

Text A

Taking Our Time Off

By Rana Foroohar and William Underhill

Warming-up Exercises

☞ Do you think traveling is a good way to relax yourself? Why or why not? What are the other ways you like to choose to spend your leisure time?

☞ Besides emission of carbon by taking airplanes what else does traveling bring to the environment?

• First reading •

Directions: Now please read the following passage as fast as you can and summarize the main idea.

1   Andrew Sims has a no-fly rule. As an international development expert and policy director for London's New Economics Foundation, he spends his days thinking globally. But when he travels on holiday, it's always closer to home; several years ago he decided never again to take a vacation by air. "The decision was partly driven by a concern for the environment," says Sims, "but it's also driven by a desire not to overlook what's on your doorstep, and to travel in a more leisurely way." Now, instead of hopping a cheap flight to Spain or the Cote d'Azur, Sims and his family board a sleeper train from London to the west coast of Scotland. They spend unstructured days amid the **lochs** and islands, hiking, cooking or just dreaming. The journey itself—made partly on a single track, which curves so that the back of the train is visible from the front—is a key part of the trip. No matter that it takes three times longer than flying; for Sims and his family, enjoying breakfast in bed while **chugging** past some of the world's most beautiful scenery is the end, not the means to get there.

2   More and more, people are living for vacation. They are using up every single allotted day off, and bargaining with their employers for more time to savor their travels. Gone are the days when holidays were a discreet, predictable part of the year; today they are more typically considered an essential, non-negotiable part of life. We transition **seamlessly** from the **drudgery** of work and responsibilities of family to the pleasures of time off—and back again. Today's trips are more-**organic** narratives, and the traveler is the storyteller. "The whole idea of 'If it's Tuesday, it must be Belize' is completely over," says Navin Sawhney, senior VP of the Connecticut-based tour operator Tauck World Discovery. "Today's tourists view travel as a form of self-expression. They don't want to come back with an object, or even a picture.

lochs *n.* a lake or a part of the sea partly enclosed by land in Scotland（苏格兰）湖，狭长的海湾
chug *v.* If a car, train, etc. chugs somewhere, it moves there slowly, with the engine making a repeated low sound 发着咔嚓声行驶
seamlessly *adv.* done or made so smoothly that you cannot tell where one thing stops and another begins 连贯地
drudgery *n.* hard boring work 苦活，单调乏味的工作
organic *adj.* happening in a natural way, without anyone planning it or forcing it to happen 自然的，纯朴的

They want to come back with a story."

3   The trend toward leisurely, in-depth holidays, like so many others stems from the baby boomers. They've worked hard—the white-collar toil has largely driven the past few years of global productivity growth—and now they have the money and the time to enjoy themselves. Travelers since they were teens, they've already seen the great museums of Europe, and probably the key monuments of Asia and the plains of Africa. Rather than zip through 20 countries in 20 days, they are more interested in hanging out in a remote corner of one, interacting with locals and **sampling** new customs. Quality and depth of experience matter far more than crossing hot spots off a checklist. This is reflected in the travel industry's new marketing campaigns, notes Alex Kyriakidis, managing partner of Deloitte's global tourism practice. "Greece invites people to 'Explore your sense,'" he says. "Intercontinental [Hotels] asks, 'Are you living an Intercontinental life?'"

4   The idea of getting there being half the fun is behind the recent boom in **chartered**-boat trips, which allow travelers to pull in and out of ports as the mood strikes. Geoffrey Kent, head of the luxe travel company Abercrombie & Kent, recently planned a six-week private Arctic diving trip aboard a small cruise ship for a well-known CEO client. "This is someone who's done everything," says Kent. "He's got his own Gulf-stream V. What he wanted was to really get away for a slow, extended vacation with his family and friends."

5   To be sure, slower doesn't necessarily mean cheaper. A **sluggish** top-of-the-range cruise on a luxury **barge** through the canals of the Netherlands will cost more than £1,600 a week. The bill for a five-day stroll through the Tuscan landscape (with luggage sent on ahead, of course) could be at least £500—before the cost of the trip to Italy. And the fare for a one-way overnight trip from Paris to Barcelona on the Elipsos service—billed as a "train hotel"—can run £250, or the price of a night in a very nice Hyatt.

6   For devotees, the biggest advantage of leisurely tourism is that slow means green. "Among my friends I find that more and more are limiting themselves to perhaps one flight a year," says Kieran. Europeans in particular are buying into low-carbon holidays; Inn-travel, a U.K.-based firm specializing in skiing and cycling holidays, says train journeys are up 50 percent over last year. Canny train operators have quickly figured out how to **flaunt**

> **sample** v. to try an activity, go to a place, etc. in order to see what it is like 尝试
> **charter** v. to pay a company for the use of their aircraft, boat, etc. 包租（飞机、轮船等）
> **sluggish** adj. moving or reacting more slowly than normal 慢吞吞的
> **barge** n. a large low boat with a flat bottom 大型平底船，驳船
> **flaunt** v. to show your money, success, beauty, etc. so that other people notice it — used to show disapproval 炫耀，夸耀

their environmental **credentials**. In France, train travelers who purchase tickets at www.voyages-sncf.com can now measure their virtue on an "Eco-Gauge." (For the record, a high-speed-train ride between Paris and Marseille will emit 10kg of carbon per passenger, compared with 187kg if traveled by plane and 313kg by car.) "Slow travel is like buying organic food," says John Kester of the World Tourist Organization in Madrid. "You might do it for ideological reasons—or because it tastes better."

> **credential** *n.* someone's education, achievements, experience, etc. that prove they have the ability to do something 某人可以得到信任的证明

7   How these new travelers—whose numbers are   yone's guess. What's clear is that traditional holidays will continue to evolve, becoming more personalized and in-depth. Among travelers, the sense of urgency—Climb Kilimanjaro before it melts away! See the Sistine Chapel before you die!—so prevalent in the workday world is fading. Despite all the fretting about climate change, the world is not going to disappear any time soon; in fact, environmental activism seems to be gaining traction. And if you missed the "Mona Lisa"? Oh well. There's always next time.

(Words: 933)

• Second Reading •

Directions: Read the text again more carefully to find enough information for Exercises I, II & III.

Exercise I   True or False

Directions: Please state whether the following statements are true or false (T/F) according to what you've found in the text.

1. The concern for the environment is the only reason why Andrew Sims chose not to travel by air.
2. For the Sims, the journey is the most important part of a trip.
3. In the past, holiday was carefully planned and travelers would bring back with them souvenirs.

4. Now some non-traditional travelers will take holiday a natural part of their lives and come back with organic food.
5. The trend of in-depth traveling stems from baby boomers because they have already visited significant scenic spots and have no interest in traveling around.
6. People charter boats to travel because they can stop whenever and wherever they want to.
7. To have a non-traditional holiday is much cheaper than visiting 20 cities in 20 days.
8. People like slow travel because it does no harm to the environment.
9. People who choose slow travel will also buy organic food.
10. It is the sense of urgency that drives people to ignore the beautiful sceneries around their doorsteps and visit lochs in Scotland.

Exercise II Word Inference

Directions: Often you can guess the meaning of a word/expression by reading the words around it. Please read the given sentence to see how each word/expression in bold type is used in the text. Then choose the answer that is closest in meaning to the bold-faced word/expression.

1. Now, instead of **hopping** a cheap flight to Spain or the Cote d'Azur, Sims and his family board a sleeper train from London to the west coast of Scotland.
   A. getting on   B. choosing
   C. preferring   D. hiring
2. They spend **unstructured** days amid the lochs and islands, hiking, cooking or just dreaming.
   A. leisure   B. delighted
   C. not well-organized   D. endless
3. They are using up every single allotted day off, and bargaining with their employers for more time to **savor** their travels.
   A. decide   B. enjoy
   C. spend on   D. fulfil
4. Rather than **zip** through 20 countries in 20 days, they are more interested in hanging out in a remote corner of one, interacting with locals and sampling new customs.
   A. whiz   B. fasten

C. move   D. go

5. A sluggish **top-of-the-range** cruise on a luxury barge through the canals of the Netherlands will cost more than £1,600 a week.

    A. slow   B. very good
    C. personal   D. private

6. And the fare for a one-way overnight trip from Paris to Barcelona on the Elipsos service—**billed** as a "train hotel"—can run £250, or the price of a night in a very nice Hyatt.

    A. registered   B. labeled
    C. paid   D. advertised

7. For **devotees**, the biggest advantage of leisurely tourism is that slow means green.

    A. someone who enjoys sth very much   B. someone who is attracted by sth
    C. someone who believes in God   D. someone who is an environmentalist

8. **Canny** train operators have quickly figured out how to flaunt their environmental credentials.

    A. considerate   B. environmental
    C. generous   D. clever

9. How these new travelers—whose numbers are only **slated** to grow—will eventually spend their time and money is anyone's guess.

    A. planned   B. doomed
    C. foreseen   D. proposed

10. Despite all the fretting about climate change, the world is not going to disappear any time soon; in fact, environmental activism seems to be gaining **traction**.

    A. industry   B. power
    C. charm   D. weight

Exercise III   Discussion

Directions: Please discuss the following questions in pairs or groups.

1. Will you choose in-depth and slow travel out of the concern for the environment?
2. Which one would you like to choose—visiting places around the world or exploring details in a few small towns? Why?
3. When you travel around, what kinds of things you like to visit and in what way?

Text B

Tourists Who Stay Close to Home

By Owen Matthews

Warming-up Exercises

☞ What changes do you think economic development in China has brought about to people's lives?

☞ Have you traveled a lot in China? Which place has left you the deepest impression?

• First reading •

Directions: Now please read the following passage as fast as you can and summarize the main idea.

1 A decade ago, hotels in princely palaces in Rajasthan, India, were the preserve of wealthy Western tourist. "The only locals you'd see were either in the fields or serving you drinks," says London lawyer Rory White, a veteran India traveler. No longer. These days, you're less likely to see Europeans than wealthy Indians at the Lake Palace in Udaipur and well-to-do Chinese at the Red Capital Ranch boutique hotel near Beijing, with its gorgeous views of the Great Wall.

2 ___A___. They've created a boom in domestic travel that has rapidly raised the level of accommodations and services. Many have traveled on package tours abroad, and are demanding the same amenities they found overseas, from spa treatments to high-thread-count sheets. And their demand for upscale travel is reaching even the most remote corners of the earth, from Tibet to Siberia, where posh hotels are opening in areas once hospitable only to backpackers. Richer tourists want "something more sophisticated than beaches and unlimited buffets," says Svetlana Gracheva of Moscow's exclusive "VIP tours" agency—and that means trips far off the beaten path, from the once forbidden old city of Lhasa to the mountains of Tuva, on the Russian-Chinese border.

3 ___B___. Currently there are 320,000 millionaires in the country, worth a total of $1.6 trillion, whose free-spending ways have driven the country's luxury-goods market to grow by

28 percent a year. And these big spenders don't just want to buy pretty things; they want to see beautiful places increasingly in their own country. Shao Qiwen, director of China's National Tourism Administration, predicts that China's tourism business will be worth a staggering $128 billion this year, much of that coming from an estimated 1.5 billion domestic travelers. Many Chinese "can afford to spend an average of $20,000 per trip per couple," boasts Lily Liu, one of the organizers of last November's first-ever China Luxury Travel Fair in Shanghai, which brought high-end hoteliers and **tony** travel providers together with prospective clients.

4 China's new elite are rediscovering an ancient local tradition: hot springs and spas. Outside Beijing's Sixth Ring Road, far from the turbulent urban **sprawl** of China's capital, I Spa provides an **oasis** of comfort and indulgence, centered on a series of **roiling** pools of mineral-rich water. Last year the spa opened a small boutique hotel called the Napa Club, featuring what the brochure calls "Californian nobleness and elegance." Though the hotel **décor** is distinctly American, the **clientele** is almost exclusively Chinese; they even have a Hunanese chef to cater to spice-loving guests from southern provinces. Napa's Escape the City package is a favorite with **beleaguered** businesswomen; it includes a **detoxifying** body scrub meant to remove the poisons that have accumulated from Beijing's polluted atmosphere.

5 _____C_____. During the winter, they flock to traditional hot spots like Egypt, Turkey and Dubai. But during the summer months, more and more Russians are returning to their own Black Sea coast, lured by cheap flights and Russian-speaking service. Old Soviet-era **sanatoriums** and resorts around Sochi and Crimea in Ukraine are being refurbished, and new hotels are springing up in anticipation of Sochi's 2014 Winter Olympic bid. But even Sergey Gorsky, director of the Moscow International Travel and Tourism Exhibition, admits that Russian destinations still have a way to go before they can truly compete. "Egypt is famous for its Red Sea, corals and pyramids, Greece for ruins, Italy for architecture," he says. "What does Russia have to offer to our middle class, spoiled by the luxury and beauty they have experienced abroad?

> **tony** adj. marked by an elegant or exclusive manner or quality 精品的，高档次的
> **sprawl** n. a large area covered with buildings that spreads from the city into the countryside in an ugly way (城市)杂乱无序拓展的地区
> **oasis** n. an area in the desert where there is water and where plants grow 绿洲
> **roiling** adj. (of a liquid) agitated vigorously; turbulent 搅浑的
> **décor** n. the style in which the inside of a building is decorated 装饰布局/风格
> **clientele** n. all the clients of a shop/store, organization, etc. 客户
> **beleaguered** adj. experiencing a lot of criticism and difficulties 处于困境的
> **detoxify** v. to remove harmful substances or poisons from sth 解毒，祛毒
> **sanatorium** n. a place like a hospital where patients who have a lasting illness or who are getting better after an illness are treated 疗养院，休养所

Sochi is not much cheaper than Turkey and service is still much worse."

6 Yet away from the overpriced beaches, Russia offers plenty of wonders that locals are starting to discover for themselves. "Russian middle-class tourists have had enough of 'all inclusive' Turkish service," says Guly Alexander, a writer for vacation to Russia magazine. "Russia can offer so many exotic treasures: hot springs in Kamchatka, sulfur springs in Caucasus, the beautiful Pacific beaches of the Far East, the mountains of the Altai." More than 200,000 Russian tourists visited Siberia's crystal-clear Lake Baikal last year—four times more than the year before—drawn by a new tourist railway along the shore and a summer **shaman** festival. __D__.

7 Other remote areas are beginning to develop their upscale tourist trades, too. Lhasa, Tibet, has three high-end hotels under construction, including the St. Regis and the Park Hyatt. The House of Shambhala Lhasa, a boutique hotel with 10 luxury rooms all done in traditional Tibetan style, opened last summer, catering to high-end Chinese traveler. It boasts a Himalayan menu combining traditional Tibetan favorites with a

> **shaman** *n.* a person in some religions and societies who is believed to be able to contact good and evil spirits and cure people of illnesses 萨满
> **trek** *n.* a long, hard walk lasting several days or weeks, especially in the mountains 长途跋涉，艰难的旅程

fusion of flavors from India, Kashmir, Nepal and western China, a teahouse, a spa and retail space for the produce of the Shambhala Foundation's culturally sustainable micro-enterprises. The Shambhala's founder, Laurence Brahm, takes pride in the fact that only local workers and materials (except for electrical wiring) were used in the construction of the hotel. Ninety percent of visitors to Lhasa are domestic travelers eager to see a part of their country that was inaccessible to most Chinese citizens for decades.

8 Travel at home is set to grow faster than any other sector of the tourism industry, according to Tourism Futures International, which studies Asian tourism trends. __E__. "My friends and I have traveled all over Europe, but we haven't seen our own country," says Sergei Dubrovsky, a Moscow-based engineer who enjoyed a **trekking** vacation this year in the mountains of the Altai. "I could spend the rest of my life traveling around my homeland, and still not see it all." But he could spend the whole time staying in high style.

(Words: 938)

Second Reading

Directions: Read the text again more carefully to find enough information for Exercises I, II, III & IV.

Exercise I Understanding Text Organization

Directions: You may find there are a few sentences (segments) missing from the passage. Read the article through and decide where the following sentences should go.

1. No country embodies the trend toward upscale domestic travel more than China, where the purchasing power of the middle class has expanded at an astonishing pace over the last decade
2. A similar number of Russians even visited Magadan, the remote far-eastern region famous only for its old gulags
3. Across Eurasia, local middle-class travelers are increasingly choosing to vacation in their own countries
4. And with so much to see in Eurasia, it's easy to understand why
5. Russian holidaymakers, understandably, look for warmth and sun

Exercise II Multiple-Choice Questions

Directions: Please choose the best answer to the following questions.

1. What do we learn from Para.1?
    A. Many wealthy people in China and India are enjoying upscale trips domestically.
    B. European travelers only see local people serving drinks while they travel in Asia as the local people are very poor.
    C. You usually see only Europeans and Americans in those luxury hotels.
    D. Western tourists do not like seeing many Asians in the travel resorts.
2. Paragraph 2 tells us that _____.
    A. travelers still like sophisticated places like beaches and buffets best
    B. it seems travelers do not like Lhasa any more
    C. wealthy travelers are looking for non-traditional places
    D. amenities are not important for travelers

3. How many millionaires are there in China according to the article?
   A. 128,000.   B. 1.5 million.
   C. 20,000.   D. 320,000.
4. Chinese middle class travelers seem to have rediscovered the pleasure of _____.
   A. spicy food   B. hot springs
   C. spas   D. both B and C
5. Besides China, people in which country/region have also begun to discover the pleasure of domestic traveling?
   A. Britain.   B. Russia.
   C. Continental Europe.   D. the US.

Exercise III Word Inference

Directions: Often you can guess the meaning of a word/expression by reading the words around it. Please read the given sentence to see how each word/expression in bold type is used in the text. Then choose the answer that is closest in meaning to the bold-faced word/expression.

1. These days, you're less likely to see Europeans than wealthy Indians at the Lake Palace in Udaipur and well-to-do Chinese at the Red Capital Ranch boutique hotel near Beijing, with its **gorgeous** views of the Great Wall.
   A. grandiose   B. famous
   C. splendid   D. infamous
2. And their demand for upscale travel is reaching even the most remote corners of the earth, from Tibet to Siberia, where **posh** hotels are opening in areas once hospitable only to backpackers.
   A. classy   B. inexpensive
   C. new   D. young
3. Shao Qiwen, director of China's National Tourism Administration, predicts that China's tourism business will be worth a **staggering** $128 billion this year, much of that coming from an estimated 1.5 billion domestic travelers.
   A. hesitating   B. stumbling
   C. faltering   D. amazing
4. Many Chinese "can afford to spend an average of $20,000 per trip per couple," boasts Lily Liu, one of the organizers of last November's first-ever China Luxury Travel Fair in Shanghai, which brought high-end hoteliers and tony travel providers together with

prospective clients.

A. proponent B. potential
C. pleasing D. eligible

5. Outside Beijing's Sixth Ring Road, far from the **turbulent** urban sprawl of China's capital, I Spa provides an oasis of comfort and indulgence, centered on a series of roiling pools of mineral-rich water.

A. violent B. disorderly
C. truthful D. troublesome

6. But during the summer months, more and more Russians are returning to their own Black Sea coast, **lured** by cheap flights and Russian-speaking service.

A. attracted B. seduced
C. opposed D. pushed up

7. Old Soviet-era sanatoriums and resorts around Sochi and Crimea in Ukraine are being **refurbished**, and new hotels are springing up in anticipation of Sochi's 2014 Winter Olympic bid.

A. rebuilt B. refreshed
C. pulled down D. redecorated

8. Russia can offer so many **exotic** treasures: hot springs in Kamchatka, sulfur springs in Caucasus, the beautiful Pacific beaches of the Far East, the mountains of the Altai.

A. tasty B. unusual
C. hot D. exciting

9. It boasts a Himalayan menu combining traditional Tibetan favorites with a **fusion** of flavors from India, Kashmir, Nepal and western China, a teahouse, a spa and retail space for the produce of the Shambhala Foundation's culturally sustainable micro-enterprises.

A. joining B. change
C. blending D. confusion

10. Ninety percent of visitors to Lhasa are domestic travelers eager to see a part of their country that was **inaccessible** to most Chinese citizens for decades.

A. impossible to reach B. expensive
C. unimaginable D. unapproachable

Exercise IV Discussion

Directions: Please discuss the following questions in pairs or groups.

1. If you are going to travel in China, which place do you want to go to first and why?
2. What do you think are the advantages and disadvantages of traveling domestically and abroad?
3. Can you introduce to your classmates one place in Europe or the US?

Text C

Capturing the Niche

By Michelle Jana Chan

1   Claire Hurren is not interested in spending her vacation lying on a beach, shopping or museum hopping. She doesn't even want to go on safari. The 32-year-old doctor from Nottinghamshire, England, hopes to do something more focused and meaningful with her time off. So this August she will head to Greece to count dolphins for a population census by Earthwatch Institute. "I want to be involved in conservation," says Hurren, who has taken 14 other Earthwatch trips, including spotlight surveys of caimans on the Amazon. "I mean, it's not that hard: you're out in a boat watching dolphins in the sunshine. And I know the money I spend on the trips is going to scientific research."

2   More than most, slow travelers vacation with a rigorous sense of purpose. They have the time, energy and attention spans to zero in on one thing, whether it's playing every golf course in Scotland, learning to paint like Michelangelo, saving the Siberian tiger or visiting their ancestral homelands, from Ireland to India. Many are driven by concerns about the environment; they understand the havoc mass-market tourism can wreak on the planet, and shun all-inclusive resorts that threaten local livelihoods and packaged tours that can trample the world's ancient and fragile monuments.

3   Recognizing the growing demand for specialized holidays, savvy tour operators are repositioning themselves to cover niche areas of the market, from Thai cooking holidays to volunteer aid programs in Africa. Companies that used to differentiate themselves on price or region are now segmenting the market even more finely, focusing on one aspect of travel. Ian Bradley, spokesperson for the Association of Independent Tour Operators, notes that as the industry has matured, so have travelers' tastes. "People are looking for something more exclusive, off the beaten track and adventurous," he says. "They want to say, 'I didn't just go to

Amsterdam for the weekend but I went whale watching in Iceland or wine tasting in South Africa.'"

4   Classic tours of culturally rich destinations are simply no longer enough. Heather Chan, general manager of the London-based tour operator CTS Horizons, says their traditional tours of Beijing and the Great Wall didn't seem to satisfy all their customers. "We were hearing feedback like, 'It's a pity we didn't have more time to talk to locals' and 'We want to feel what it's like to live in the country'." So last year the company introduced a new tour to Wuzhen, a historic cobbled town outside Shanghai, which included classes in Chinese painting and calligraphy, cooking lessons and sessions with a traditional Chinese doctor. 'Tourists want to experience authentic local life—and to do it more leisurely," Chan says.

5   Creating an experience for travelers who share the same interest creates a sense of community—and that keeps customers coming back. Las och Res, a Swedish tour operator that specializes in rural vacations in non-Western countries, says that nearly two thirds of guests make a repeat booking. Las och Res uses home-stay accommodations in villages and prepares travelers with generous packets of literature in advance of their trips, so they can better relate to locals they meet. At roughly three weeks each, they're also longer than the average tour. "Travelers need time to have in-depth meetings with local people," says founder Christian Jutvik. "Second class on an Indian train is always going to be more interesting than an air-conditioned tourist coach." Anke Samulowitz, a 41-year-old health manager from Stockholm, has traveled with Las och Res five times, from Haiti to Indonesia. And she has made friends for life. "The people who go on these trips think similarly," Samulowitz says. "I met two girls on a trip to Equatorial Guinea and we kept in touch and decided to go to India together."

6   Some highly specialized tours grew out of other niches. Kenyan Chris Food, 36, founded Footstep Safaris in Nairobi two years ago to provide bespoke tours around East Africa. He also offers spiritual and Christian-based safaris to his offerings, which have proved very popular. "I thought there was a niche for people with lots of cash who wanted top-end safaris but didn't feel like they had to leave their spiritual life behind," says Foot. "This is luxury within the context of faith." Guests can experience communion in the bush, visit local Christian communities and pause beneath an acacia tree for a moment of reflection during a morning game drive. "I'm bringing together Dom Perignon with prayers," says Foot. "They're not mutually exclusive." Foot is also planning to offer investment opportunities to guests in ethics and fair-trade enterprise, linking First World financing to local people in need. "Nowadays, people want to be doing something more than just go on holiday," he says.

7   That's an increasingly common refrain. CC Africa has been offering more than just

vacations for over 10 years. With more than 40 high-end camps and lodges across Africa and India, it is a leading operator in sustainable ecotourism, organizing tourists to take walking safaris in the bush and visit local schools and villages. Ron Magill, a 47-year-old media director from the Miami zoo and a longtime champion of the company, is just back from spotting tigers at Mahua Kothi Lodge in Madhya Pradesh, India. "CC Africa is out there to save the environment. They believe if we give back to the local communities, those people will in turn look after the wildlife," he says. "That's the reason I choose them. They build their decks around trees; they don't cut down trees."

8   Don't discount the luxury, though, says Nicky Fitzgerald, marketing director at CC Africa's Johannesburg headquarters. "Of course what attracts people to us in the first place is the bedrooms, the plunge pools, the 'best hotel in the world' by Conde Nast," she says. "But then we stand out from the rest by our community work. Our guests can visit clinics and see rows of HIV-positive mothers. More and more, they want to see their dollar making a difference." Often they return home with a new sense of commitment. Magill is currently raising money for a conservation project he witnessed on his India vacation: "I'm getting ready to send $5,000 to a sloth-bear rehabilitation project that I saw when I was out there," he says.

9   Earthwatch Institute takes interactive conservation even further: it recruits guests to join scientists in field research, like the trips that Hurren took. Such volunteer vacations are competitive with regular vacations; 13 days tracking koalas in Australia cost $2,470—including accommodations, food and activities. Earthwatch Europe has seen a 68 percent rise in volunteers in the last 10 years, and its global repeat rate for guests is 50 percent. Nigel Winser, Earthwatch Europe's executive director, says more people than ever are interested in using their vacation time in other ways. "It's an opportunity to get away, learn about the environment and give something back," he says.

10 Some tourists prefer to leave the environmental activism to the resorts they choose. Six Senses, which owns nine luxury properties across Asia, is known as one of the top innovators in adopting environmental initiatives. "Every property has its own resident environmentalist, and we're constantly trying out new technology to become more sustainable," says Sonu Shivdasani, who founded the company 12 years ago with his wife, Eva. "We're cultivating dragonflies to kill mosquitoes and cooling villas by pumping cold seawater through fan units. Next year we're opening a luxury eco-suite at Soneva Kiri in Thailand, which will be carbon zero. It will have natural ventilation, solar-powered air conditioning and a small windmill for electricity. That's what we believe 21st-century travelers really want." And if that's what they want, there are plenty of businesses that will be only too happy to give it to them.

(Words: 1285)

Exercise I Discussion

Directions: Please discuss the following questions in pairs or groups.

1. Do you prefer touring a place by following a tight schedule fixed by tourism agency, or just go alone with your family members?
2. Do you want to spend more money riding first class, staying in up-scale hotels and dining in restaurants for high-end tourists? Why/why not?
3. Do you want to visit local families and see how they live by staying with them for a couple of days? Why/why not?

Exercise II Writing

Directions: The articles in this unit are related tourism; write a composition in about 200 words about an unforgettable trip to a scenic attraction or a historic site; or give your suggestions for improvement where you find something not quite to your taste or your belief.

UNIT FOUR

BUSINESS AND FINANCE

Target of the Unit

☞ To get a glimpse of some aspects of modern business and consumption patterns
☞ To practice reading skills
☞ To enlarge your vocabulary

1) LEAD IN

Directions: In this unit, you will read 3 passages about business practices, habits of consumption and problems existing in an economy. As you read think of those elements that propel a modern society to move forward.

2) DISCUSSION

Have you heard about the Lenovo-IBM merging? What are the advantages and disadvantages of merging between businesses?

Text A

Land of the Giants

By Daren Fonda

Warming-up Exercises

☞ What do you know about a consumer society?
☞ What does CPI mean to you?

• First reading •

Directions: Now please read the following passage as fast as you can and summarize the main idea.

1 Forget the accounting scandals, the CEOs fending off fraud charges, the **churning** stock market. The business world has become obsessed with corporate nuptials. Merger **mania** is back, executives are cashing out and, if history is any guide, investors should be running for cover. A couple of months ago, Kmart and Sears got engaged. Then Nextel and Sprint announced their $35 billion wedding. Johnson & Johnson is buying Guidant, a maker of medical devices, for $24 billion. Two of the splashiest deals came last week: SBC, the Baby Bell based in San Antonio, Texas, looked poised to swallow its former parent, AT&T, in a deal that could top $15 billion. Then Procter & Gamble said it would acquire Gillette for $57 billion, forging a consumer-products giant with brands ranging from Gillette's Right Guard deodorant and Mach3 razors to P&G Crest, Pampers and Tide.

> **churning** *adj.* moving about violently 动荡的
> **mania** *n.* a strong desire for something or interest in something, especially one that affects a lot of people at the same time; craze 狂热
> **hype** *n.* attempts to make people think something is good or important by talking about it a lot on television, the radio, etc. used to show disapproval 炒作
> **write-off** *n.* an official agreement that someone does not have to pay a debt 免除债务的声明

2 For all the talk of profits and synergies, investors would be wise to view these deals with a wary eye. Blockbuster mergers tend to be duds for stockholders of the acquiring company. In seven of the nine mergers valued at more than $50 billion, the acquirer's share price is down an average of 46% from pre-merger levels, according to Fact Set Mergerstat, a research firm in Santa Monica, California. Maybe you already knew that if you're a longtime owner of Hewlett-Packard, whose stock has flat-lined since the company acquired Compaq in 2002. AOL's merger with Time Warner (parent company of TIME) may have set a new standard of paired futility, erasing some 80% of the merged company's stock value.

After the **hype** subsides, more often than not, investors wind up with tax **write-offs**.

3   Yet that hasn't slowed the latest blitz of deals. December 2004 saw $147 billion in mergers vs. $41 billion a year earlier, according to Thomson Financial. In January an additional $150 billion worth was announced. A recent survey by Bank of America Business Capital found that 23% of chief financial officers expect to do a major deal this year.

4   Why the shopping spree? In part, it's a self-perpetuation cycle. Once a few big companies in an industry join forces, everyone else feels compelled to hook up. (In consumer products, the betting now is that Kimberly-Clark and Colgate will be next.) The buying binge is also being fueled by rising stock prices—and the loads of cash piling up on corporate balance sheets. The S&P 500 is up 40% from its 2002 low, and companies in the index are sitting on $2.3 trillion in cash. Writing **dividend** checks is one way to spend the largesse. Microsoft paid $32 billion on dividends last year, and dividends are expected to rise 10% on average this year. Many executives, though, are cracking open the piggy bank and looking for acquisition targets. P&G, for instance, is using its stock to acquire Gillette, but it also plans to spend up to $22 billion to buy back shares to support the merged firm's stock price.

> **dividend** *n.* a part of a company's profit that is divided among the people with shares in the company 红利
> **groom** *v.* to take care of your own appearance by keeping your hair and clothes clean and tidy 修饰个人外貌和衣着
> **formidable** *adj.* very powerful or impressive, and often frightening 强大的，令人畏惧的

5   Investors in Gillette, headquartered in Boston, can't complain. Their shares were already up sharply over the past year, even before the 18% premium that P&G's bid provides. CEO James Kilts, for one, stands to make an estimated $123 million from selling his firm to P&G, based on last week's stock prices and options that will vest when the ink on the deal dries. Famed investor Warren Buffett has also scored big, reaping a paper profit of $567 million for Berkshire Hathaway, which owns 96 million Gillette shares. "It's a dream deal," he said in a statement, pledging to raise his stake to 100 million shares as a vote of confidence.

6   But what about P&G shareholders? While Wall Street has reacted coolly to some recent mergers (investors pummeled software firm Symantec after it announced a $13.5 billion bid for Veritas), the assessment on this one has been largely positive. P&G chief executive A.G. Lafley has argued that the combination will rev up sales of Gillette's men's **grooming** line, particularly in markets like China, where P&G is strongly embedded, and Procter's business stands to gain from Gillette's **formidable** operations in countries like India and Brazil. "Together, P&G and Gillette could grow at levels neither of us could sustain on our own," Lafley told investors last week. Specifically, he and Kilts (who will stay on as a P&G vice chairman) pledged to squeeze $14 billion to $16 billion in "revenue and cost synergies" out of

the firm.

7   Sounds pretty good, but do the numbers add up? With few overlapping products, neither company was talking last week about cutting lines of goods. As for job cuts, the plan calls for eliminating a relatively small number—6,000 of the combined firm's 140,000 employees worldwide. That won't save billions. Another argument from deal enthusiasts: the merger will give the firms greater bargaining **clout** with big retail chains. "This is a response to the Wal-Martization of America," says Joseph Altobello, an analyst at CIBC World Markets. A similar case is made regarding advertising purchases—that together the brand-swollen behemoth will be able to wring more favorable terms for ads. Yet P&G and Gillette were megafirms separately. How much more leverage can they truly gain?

8   The hardest advantage to measure is that merger **buzzword** synergy. "P&G knows a lot about women. Gillette knows a lot about men," Lafley told investors. "It's very simple, but it's a potent combination." Robert McDonald, a P&G senior executive, hinted to TIME at new products that could capitalize on each firm's strengths. "We have the best-selling male fragrance in Hugo Boss," he says. "How about a Hugo Boss designer razor?" Problem is, with P&G already so big, boasting more than $50 billion in sales, it needs the equivalent of a new mega-brand like Tide each year to hit its targets of 5% to 7% annual growth. That would be a lot of Boss razors.

> **clout** *n.* power or the authority to influence other people's decisions 力量，影响
> **buzzword** *n.* a word or phrase from one special area of knowledge that people suddenly think is very important 热点词，时髦词语

9   So, will bigger be better? Unlike the mates in the HP-Compaq and AOL-Time Warner deals, both partners here are marrying from positions of strength. P&G, for one, has had several recent hits, like Crest Whitestrips and Swiffer cleaning products, and Wall Street loves Lafley for increasing operating income and turbo-charging the growth of brands like Iams pet food (another acquisition). On the other hand, P&G has never absorbed a company as large as Gillette, with its 30,000 employees, and the price it's paying is steep. "We are skeptical that simply going from $55 billion to $65 billion in revenues really changes all that much," wrote J.P. Morgan analyst John Faucher in a note to investors last week. We'll know when the honeymoon ends.

(Words: 1105)

• Second Reading •

Directions: Read the text again more carefully to find enough information for Exercises I, II & III.

Exercise I True or False

Directions: Please state whether the following statements are true or false (T/F) according to what you've found in the text.

1. The present trend of merging is favorable for executives and investors.
2. More often than not, the acquirer's share price will decrease after the acquisition.
3. The undesirable share price has slowed down the merging fever.
4. The only reason that led to the present merging mania is the "follow the Joneses" mentality.
5. The stock market is a bull and businesses are making big profit now.
6. P&G is doing extremely well in markets like India and Brazil.
7. It is probable that the merger of P&G and Gillette will not affect many of their lines of product, or a large number of employees worldwide.
8. After P&G and Gillette merges, the author believes they will make more favorable terms for ads.
9. The author is optimistic about the future of a designer razor by the merger.
10. It is implied in the text that in the HP-Compaq and AOL-Time Warner deals, the two parties were not merged from positions of strength.

Exercise II Word Inference

Directions: Often you can guess the meaning of a word/expression by reading the words around it. Please read the given sentence to see how each word/expression in bold type is used in the text. Then choose the answer that is closest in meaning to the bold-faced word/expression.

1. The business world has become obsessed with corporate **nuptials**.
   A. weddings   B. scandals
   C. reports   D. management

2. Two of the splashiest deals came last week: SBC, the Baby Bell based in San Antonio, Texas, looked **poised** to swallow its former parent, AT&T, in a deal that could top $15 billion.
   A. anxious			B. happy
   C. ready			D. vicious

3. For all the talk of profits and **synergies**, investors would be wise to view these deals with a wary eye.
   A. gains			B. losses
   C. co-ordinations		D. successes

4. The buying **binge** is also being fueled by rising stock prices—and the loads of cash piling up on corporate balance sheets.
   A. plan			B. spree
   C. power			D. trend

5. CEO James Kilts, for one, stands to make an estimated $123 million from selling his firm to P&G, based on last week's stock prices and options that will **vest** when the ink on the deal dries.
   A. put on garments		B. drop
   C. rise			D. be the expected benefit

6. While Wall Street has reacted coolly to some recent mergers (investors **pummeled** software firm Symantec after it announced a $13.5 billion bid for Veritas), the assessment on this one has been largely positive.
   A. gave a warm welcome	B. rushed to buy
   C. struck			D. panicked

7. P&G chief executive A.G. Lafley has argued that the combination will **rev up** sales of Gillette's men's grooming line, particularly in markets like China, where P&G is strongly embedded, and Procter's business stands to gain from Gillette's formidable operations in countries like India and Brazil.
   A. increase			B. decrease
   C. stop			D. hinder

8. A similar case is made regarding advertising purchases—that together the brand-swollen **behemoth** will be able to wring more favorable terms for ads.
   A. attempt			B. giant
   C. agency			D. company

9. "It's very simple, but it's a **potent** combination." Robert McDonald, a P&G senior executive, hinted to TIME at new products that could capitalize on each firm's strengths.
   A. difficult			B. powerful

C. complex   D. uncertain
10. On the other hand, P&G has never absorbed a company as large as Gillette, with its 30,000 employees, and the price it's paying is **steep**.
    A. very low   B. very desirable
    C. reasonable   D. very high

Exercise III Discussion
Directions: Please discuss the following questions in pairs or groups.

1. Can you think of some of the problems that might be brought about this merging trend in business?
2. How will the merge between P&G-Gillette affect the Chinese consumers as well as the Chinese manufacturers?

Text B

China on Credit
By Nellie Huang

Warming-up Exercises

☞ Do you use any of the bank cards? Is it a debit or a credit card? What are some of the problems of using a credit card?
☞ Do you agree with the idea of "spending tomorrow's money today?"

• First reading •

Directions: Now please read the following passage as fast as you can and summarize the main idea.

1   Na Qiao, a 26-year-old Shanghai advertising account manager, has heard old proverbs like "Free from debt is free from care" and "A good debt is not as good as no debt" since she

was a girl—maxims she cheerfully ignores now that she's an adult with a $20,000 annual salary. Na recently financed her purchase of a $17,500 car (the down payment was 10%) and she says she uses her China Merchants Bank MasterCard "everywhere—at convenience stores, grocery store, department stores, even when I go to bars."

2   The Confucian value of thrift may be deeply rooted in Chinese culture, but Na's generation is learning to live by a new proverb: ___A___. Last year, American Express, Citigroup and HSBC all launched their first credit-card programs in mainland China, while GMAC, the financing arm of General Motors, set up shop in Shanghai, becoming the first foreign auto-finance firm in the country. These companies are salivating at the prospect of introducing the joys of borrowing to what MasterCard reckons is an emerging demographic of 45 million-60 million increasingly affluent Chinese household. So far, they've made barely a dent in this alluring market: of the 668 million cards circulating in the mainland today, only 5 million are true revolving credit cards, the kind that allow consumers to pay off purchases over time. The rest are mostly debit cards—essentially glorified ATM cards. ___B___. "The potential for consumer-credit growth is massive," says Christian Weidemann, chief of GMAC's China operations.

3   Still, China has a long way to go before it **mutates** into a nation of carefree, Western-style borrowers. ___C___, most people have little experience of managing personal debt—and that presents a risk to borrowers and lenders alike. "When you look at the growth of credit in any country, you have to look at the culture," says Alex Boorman, an analyst with Datamonitor, a London-based market-research firm. "Not having had access to credit previously means there will be hurdles. You have to make it clear that loans must be

> **mutate** *n.* an alteration or change, as in nature, form, or quality 演变
> **default** *n.* failure to perform a task or fulfill an obligation, especially failure to meet a financial obligation 未履行债务，拖欠
> **kick-start** *v.* to do sth to help a process or activity start or develop more quickly 使启动

paid off and there will be penalties if they aren't." Last year, a car-buying binge in China was soon followed by a wave of **defaults**. Although reliable statistics of the phenomenon are hard to come by, the information office of China's State Council reported that as of mid-2004, more than half of all auto loans in the mainland were in default. (In the U.S., about one out of 50 car buyers stop loan payments.)

4   ___D___. To **kick-start** domestic consumption in the late 1990s, Seoul began encouraging credit-card use by offering tax deductions for purchases made with plastic. Thousands of South Koreans went on a borrowing binge, only to get in over their heads. Several of the

country's largest card companies had to be restructured when loans totaling more than $2.5 billion soured and the economy slumped. Boorman warns: "There is the opportunity for something similar to happen [in China] if decent credit-checking procedures are not put in place."

5   Working with Chinese banks, companies like MasterCard are hoping to do just that. "From risk control to **collateral**, we're trying to bring the best practices of Western society to China," says Willie Fung, MasterCard Greater China general manager. The firm has also **collaborated** with banks and newspapers to raise public awareness about consumer debt, and offers training in personal financial management to college students.

> **collateral** *n.* property or other goods that you promise to give someone if you cannot pay back the money they lend you 抵押
> **collaborate** *v.* to work together with a person or group in order to achieve something, especially in science or art 合作
> **make a dent** *v. phr.* an appreciable consequence (especially a lessening) 影响，结果
> **void** *n.* a situation in which sth important or interesting is needed or wanted, but does not exist 空白

6   But it could still take many years for the credit-card culture to displace the Confucian aversion to debt. Fung says the average outstanding balance of revolving credit cards in China today is only $111. By contrast, the average U.S. household carries $7,519 in revolving debt. "People are somewhat cautious" on the mainland, he says. Even Na Qiao, the Shanghai ad exec, pays off her balance in full every month. ___E___.

(Words: 674)

• Second Reading •

Directions: Read the text again more carefully to find enough information for Exercises I, II, III & IV.

Exercise I   Understanding Text Organization

Directions: You may find there are a few sentences (segments) missing from the passage. Read the article through and decide where the following sentences should go.

1. Given this void

2. "In China," she says, "there is still a saying: if you don't have the money, don't spend it"

59

3. Even in a sophisticated international city like Shanghai
4. Consumer-credit companies and the Chinese government are trying to avoid the mistakes South Korea made
5. "Buy now, pay later"

Exercise II Multiple-Choice Questions
Directions: Complete each of the following statements with the best choice given.

1. It can be inferred from the first paragraph that nowadays young Chinese _____.
    A. like borrowing money from others
    B. hate borrowing money from others
    C. spend money in the same way as their ancestors
    D. spend money more carefully than their ancestors

2. All of the following statements are true EXCEPT _____.
    A. General Motors will allow people to buy their cars on credit in China.
    B. People can apply for credit cards from some foreign banks in China now.
    C. There are more credit cards than debit cards used in China.
    D. The increasingly rich Chinese households make China a huge potential market for credit spending.

3. The phenomenon in paragraph 3 indicates that _____.
    A. Chinese people are not suitable for credit spending
    B. the Chinese culture is one factor attributing to the loan default in China
    C. there are more Americans who stopped loan payments than Chinese
    D. Chinese people are embracing the new credit culture quickly

4. What is NOT the measure to take to help people use their credit cards properly?
    A. Offer tax deductions.
    B. Check their credit history carefully.
    C. Take measures such as risk control and collateral.
    D. Raise public awareness about consumer debt and offer training.

5. What's the author's opinion on the Chinese credit spending?
    A. They are happy to welcome the new means of money spending.
    B. They are very cautious in credit spending and are unwilling to owe the bank money.
    C. They are very reluctant to use tomorrow's money today.
    D. They are still looking on to decide whether to join in the joy of credit spending.

Exercise III Word Inference

Directions: Often you can guess the meaning of a word/expression by reading the words around it. Please read the given sentence to see how each word/expression in bold type is used in the text. Then choose the answer that is closest in meaning to the bold-faced word/expression.

1. Na Qiao, a 26-year-old Shanghai advertising account manager, has heard old proverbs like "Free from debt is free from care" and "A good debt is not as good as no debt" since she was a girl—**maxims** she cheerfully ignores now that she's an adult with a $20,000 annual salary.

   A. poverty   B. sayings
   C. scares   D. teachings

2. The Confucian value of **thrift** may be deeply rooted in Chinese culture, but Na's generation is learning to live by a new proverb: …

   A. misery   B. generosity
   C. careful use of money   D. lavishness

3. These companies are **salivating** at the prospect of introducing the joys of borrowing to what MasterCard reckons is an emerging demographic of 45 million-60 million increasingly affluent Chinese household.

   A. yearning for   B. planning
   C. working hard   D. enjoying

4. These companies are salivating at the prospect of introducing the joys of borrowing to what MasterCard reckons is an emerging **demographic** of 45 million-60 million increasingly affluent Chinese household.

   A. phenomenon   B. demonstration
   C. trend   D. group of people

5. So far, they've made barely a dent in this **alluring** market: of the 668 million cards circulating in the mainland today, only 5 million are true revolving credit cards, the kind that allow consumers to pay off purchases over time.

   A. very attractive   B. huge
   C. desirable   D. emerging

6. Still, China has a long way to go before it **mutates** into a nation of carefree, Western-style borrowers.

   A. develops   B. evolves
   C. shift   D. transforms

7. Not having had access to credit previously means there will be **hurdles**.

   A. delays B. obstacles
   C. unwillingness D. ignorance

8. Thousands of South Koreans went on a borrowing binge, only to **get in over their heads**.

   A. be drowned B. get into trouble
   C. feel very happy D. get a headache

9. Several of the country's largest card companies had to be restructured when loans totaling more than $2.5 billion soured and the economy **slumped**.

   A. fell into recession B. recovered
   C. suffered D. turned good

10. But it could still take many years for the credit-card culture to displace the Confucian **aversion** to debt.

    A. concern B. warning
    C. worry D. hatred

Exercise IV   Discussion

Directions: Please discuss the following questions in pairs or groups.

1. What do you think of Na Qiao's lifestyle? Do you prefer to have it now on installment, or save to buy it in the future?

2. What do you think of the overall situation of credit spending in China? Will this situation change over time? How will this affect our life?

3. Do you think the Confucian teachings will play some role in restraining the Chinese from spending the money they don't have?

Text C

The Irish Question

By Jim Ledbetter

1   The main street of Leixlip in county Kildare looks as if it hasn't changed for decades. There are a handful of pubs, framed with cheerfully painted woodwork and festooned with

neatly kept flower boxes. There are a newsagent, a few Chinese takeout places, a betting parlor and shops—many with the pebble-dash storefronts so familiar in the Irish countryside—to buy carpet, tiles and other household fixtures. On summer nights, local teenagers sit on benches and stone walls, much as their parents did. While the population of 15,000 makes the town the largest in the county, there is not movie theater, mall or McDonald's to hang out at.

2   And yet half a mile up the road on the outskirts of town sits one of the most sophisticated manufacturing facilities in the world. The Intel Ireland campus, built on a 150-hectare plot of land that was once a horse farm, has been in operation since 1993, approximately the year that the Irish economy turned into the famed "Celtic Tiger". Since then, Intel has invested some $7 billion, and the facility has produced more than a billion microchips. The factory has 5,500 people on the payroll, making it the largest private employer in Ireland. Instead of being a bedroom community for Dublin, a mere 17 km to the east, Leixlip has a good number of Intel workers who live in Dublin and commute here. Earlier this year, the plant began making Intel's most important product offering since the Pentium chip, using 65-namometer manufacturing processing and allowing for yet more data to be stored on yet tinier pieces of silicon.

3   The Leixlip factory is by far the largest in Europe—remarkable, given that the entire population of Ireland, just over 4 million, is about half the size of London's, or just a little bigger than Berlin's. Intel itself can hardly fathom the success. "Could we have ever forecast such phenomenal growth?" asks Trevor Holmes, Intel Ireland's head of government and public affairs. "I don't think so."

4   The growth of Intel inside Ireland echoes the explosion of Ireland's economy as a whole. In the 12 years up to 1993, the economy expanded an accumulative 60%, or the equivalent of 2.4% annually. In the 10 years after 1993, the economy grew a cumulative 96%, the equivalent of a whopping 7% a year. European Union subsidies and foreign investors—including Bristol-Myers Squibb, Dell, HP, Microsoft, eBay and SAP—have provided much of the momentum, but the Irish have benefited enormously. As recently as 1985, nearly 1 Irish worker in 5 was out of work; today unemployment stands at 4%, by most definitions full employment. Ireland boasts the highest per capita gross domestic product (GDP) in the E.U.: nearly

$41,000.

5   Such numbers are staggering to those who remember the recent past, the brain-drain year of the '70s and '80s, when anyone with talent fled Ireland as quickly as possible. Today the streets of Dublin are clogged with tourists and well-to-do locals, who flock to shopping meccas like Henry Street or, on the edge of the capital, the Liffey Valley Shopping Center, a 90-store mall. The brain drain has reversed into a brain gain; many Irish emigrants to the U.S. are returning, and so many Poles have moved here that it's common to hear Polish spoken in the local pub.

6   Just how long can the Celtic Tiger roar? And what can be done to sustain the growth? Those are the kinds of questions that keep economic-development officials from Singapore to India to the Czech Republic awake at night. In July, Davy, a brokerage affiliated with the Bank of Ireland, predicted that economic growth will begin slowing in 2008. The well-respected Economic and Social Research Institute reached a nearly identical conclusion.

7   The rationale for a slowdown is straightforward and persuasive: Ireland's housing boom, which has played an outsize role in the overall economic saga, cannot be sustained. The Davy report notes that more than 20 houses per 1,000 people will be built in 2006—four times the European average. "We can't go on building houses the way we do," insists John McGinley, a member of Kildare County Council, which includes Leixlip. Moreover, a government-backed savings-incentive plan, largely believed to have stimulated consumer demand, is due to expire next year.

8   Behind any statistical argument lurks a fear that a sustained period of growth like the one Ireland has enjoyed is a freak of economic nature. Skeptics maintain that the Celtic Tiger is suffering from a "Dutch disease"—that is, a temporary spurt comparable to Holland's discovery of offshore natural gas resources in the 1960s, which created a boom that diverted other economic activity—and then dried up. "Ireland's oil find was foreign direct investments in the late 1980s," says Danny McCoy, chief economist of the Irish Business and Employers Confederation. Others, however, believe that the tiger can stay on the prowl. "It's unduly pessimistic to project declining growth in the medium term," argues Dermot O'Brien, head of economic research at NCB Stockbrokers. He believes that native **demographic** growth and immigration will drive enough demand to keep the economy booming at least until 2020.

9   Who's right? The answer may depend on understanding how Ireland's unprecedented recovery was born. There's no single explanation; rather, government policies combined with natural strengths. One policy choice made a huge difference: in 1973, under the leadership of Prime Minister Jack Lynch, Ireland joined the European Economic Community (which later became part of the European Union). The choice was relatively uncontroversial at the time—a

referendum passed (just shy of a 5-to-1 ratio)—but it was arguably the best economic decision Ireland made in the 20th century. Joining the E.U. paved the way for economic integration with Europe and the adoption of the euro in 2002. Membership led to a massive infusion of E.U. cash as well--$3 billion in farm subsidies alone last year. Conversion to the continental currency also helped bring down interest rates, which had reached upwards of 17% in the early 1980s, in part by removing revaluation as a monetary tool.

10   Second, under Prime Minister Sean Lemass, the protectionist Irish government began opening itself up. Even so, as late as 1979, David McWilliams notes in his lively book *The Pope's Children: Ireland's New Elite*, kids on the country's east coast could not buy iconic brands of candy (like Opal Fruits) that they saw advertised on English TV—not because the sweets were bad for their teeth but because the government was determined to prop up domestic confectioners. Gradually, import restrictions were lifted, corporate tax rates were lowered—from 50% in the 1980s to 12.5% in 2003—and the government began to pursue outside investment in earnest.

11   From a U.S. multinational's point of view, these policies augmented other attractive qualities. At the same time, U.S. firms believed that doing business in Fortress Europe was going to require a physical presence there. Relatively high wages and plentiful red tape made France and West Germany unappealing. By contrast, Ireland's English-speaking workforce, surfeit of engineers and relatively low wage costs were a magnet. Still, "it took quite a bit to persuade Intel that Ireland could do it," recalls Sean Dorgan, chief executive of Ireland's Industrial Development Agency. "Part of that persuasion was showing them how many Irish electronics engineers were in places like Eindhoven and Munich with Philips and Siemens."

12   That argument, lubricated by tax incentives worth millions, persuaded Intel, along with other tech firms, to choose Ireland. The Celtic Tiger was born. And it wasn't just computer and Internet-related companies but a whole range of firms that needed a skilled workforce. Most of them were from outside (such as Procter & Gamble and Georgia Pacific), but there have been homegrown flyers as well, like Elan Pharmaceuticals, a biotech and drug company based in Dublin.

13   The ferocious expansion of the economy allowed Ireland to gloss over some of its weaknesses, like a very patchy infrastructure. Nearly every aspect of Irish life has been affected: more cars, more tourists, better restaurants, fancier homes. "We are richer than any of us imagined possible 10 years ago," says McWilliams. While many Continental European countries struggle to juice their economies, Ireland keeps racking up wins—and jobs. Last fall the pharmaceutical giant Wyeth officially opened an 111,000-sq-m biotech manufacturing facility in South County Dublin. The plant, known as Grange Castle, represents a $1.5 billion

investment and will employ 1,000 people.

14   Such continuing successes have not prevented a chorus of doubters from warning that the good times will end. Troubling signs are easy to find. There's no way that foreign direct investment (FDI) was ever going to maintain the rocket-fueled pace of the 1990s. In recent years, U.S. Treasury and tax officials have been trying to rein in corporate cost-sharing plans that allow multinationals to transfer revenues on intellectual-property assets—such as software licenses—to low-tax countries like Ireland. Moreover, new E.U. countries like Poland and the Czech Republic are winning the eye of foreign investors. As a result of these factors, plus the continuing strength of the euro, FDI in Ireland peaked in 2002 and has declined since.

15   The housing market has been dangerously overheated. An existing house in Ireland in 1993 cost, on average, just over $83,000. In 2006 that figure has skyrocketed to $471,000. As far back as 2000, the International Monetary Fund was warning that there was no precedent for such growth without a serious crash. Not surprisingly, real estate inflation also means a huge accumulation of red ink; household debt as a proportion of disposable income in Ireland has risen in the past five years to a dangerous 140%. The implications are obvious, and familiar: any economic hiccup could force consumers to stop spending.

16   That's one of the main reasons the Davy report believes that the Celtic Tiger will take a catnap. Davy's most optimistic scenario predicts growth will slow to 3.25% annually in 2009 and 2010—still quite good by European standards—but its pessimistic scenario predicts a 5% annual drop in housing prices and GDP growth of just 1%. Bulls like O'Brien argue that population growth alone should be enough to keep the expansion on track. His report predicts that, thanks to Ireland's late baby boom and open immigration policy, the country will reach 5 million citizens by 2015 and 6 million by 2050. "That demand will continue to be a major driver," he insists.

17   Can the government do anything to keep the party going? It's planning to plow more money into research and development—and give more tax credits to companies that do the same—while focusing on innovative sectors like nanotechnology and regenerative medicine. "We want new products, new services, new ways of doing things emanating from this research," says Micheal Martin, Ireland's Minister for Enterprise, Trade and Employment. Moreover, even U.S. firms that have helped Ireland blossom recognize that Ireland needs to create more of its own global companies, along the lines of the Kerry Group, a Tralee-based food-ingredients company that enjoyed $5.6 billion in revenues in 2005.

18   In the meantime, though, people in Leixlip and the rest of the country seem thankful that they have got Intel inside—and hope that their house values hold up.

(Words:1904)

Exercise I   Discussion

Directions: Please discuss the following questions in pairs or groups.

1. What are the reasons for the economic recovery of Ireland?
2. What are the worries concerning the economy of Ireland?
3. Compare the Irish and Chinese economy from what you know about the two countries.

Exercise II   Writing

Directions: Write a composition about any one of the above-related topics like the growth of a big company, the benefits of using credit cards or a comparison between two different economies in about 200 words.

UNIT FIVE

CHINA REPORT

*T*arget of the Unit

☞ To get a glimpse of the development of China over the past thirty years
☞ To practice reading skills
☞ To enlarge your vocabulary

1) LEAD IN

Directions: *In this unit, you will read 3 passages about various aspects of social life of the Chinese people. Take note of their achievements and problems they are facing.*

2) DISCUSSION

Do you prefer to travel by rail, road, air or water? Why?

Text A

All Aboard

By Melinda Liu

*W*arming-up Exercises

☞ Do you still remember what had happened a week before China entered into its Year of Rat? Did you have similar experience in your life?
☞ What do you think we should do to solve the problem of mass transit in a populous country such as China?

• First reading •

Directions: Now please read the following passage as fast as you can and summarize the main idea.

1   China is a nation on the move—especially now, at the beginning of the much-awaited Spring Festival vacation. Also known as Chinese New Year, and based on the lunar calendar, this is the longest and most popular holiday of the year. And in China, big means really big. Many of the country's 100 million-plus rural-born migrant workers leave, or even quit, jobs in the city and travel to the countryside to spend the first day of the lunar new year with family.

2   They're on the move already, armies of migrants carrying massive suitcases and cloth bundles —often balanced on shoulder poles—bulging with clothes, toys, electric appliances and other gifts for relatives back home. Hundreds of millions of such family reunions are scheduled for the period from Jan. 14 to Feb. 22, during which time more than 2 billion journeys will be made by rail, road, air and water. Some 700,000 buses will be on the road. Three hundred extra trains are being laid on to help cope with the anticipated 144 million rail journeys—an average of 3.6 million trips a day.

> **stranded** *adj.* a person or vehicle that is stranded is unable to move from the place where they are 搁浅的，被困的，未得到帮助的

3   Talk about traffic jams. Less than a week ago, heavy snowstorms hit the central Chinese province of Henan, paralyzing rail traffic on some of the country's most heavily traveled north-south routes. The following day 100,000 passengers were **stranded** at Beijing's main

railway station, and thousands of other disgruntled travelers packed stations in Zhengzhou and Shanghai. On Monday, 15,000 passengers were delayed up to 24 hours in Shanghai, waiting for 17 trains held up by the snow. Shanghai saw a fourth day of chaos on Tuesday as 10,000 stranded passengers—some of whom used nearby underground parking garages and Internet cafes as ad hoc waiting rooms—crowded around the train station.

4   Rail is still the preferred mode of travel for most of China's 1.3 billion people. The majority of travelers during this holiday period are migrant workers "who have to travel between 1,000 and 2,000 kilometers [600-1,200 miles] from their workplaces to their hometowns," says Prof. Yang Hao of the Beijing Communications University. "This is the largest human migration in the world, especially by rail."

5   China's travelers differ from those in many foreign countries, where most people prefer to go by air for long distances and by road for short distances, says Yang. Chinese rail travel is cheaper—and safer—than traveling by car. Even though China has only eight vehicles per 1,000 people, it has one of the world's highest rates of automobile fatalities. The trains are also far more affordable than air travel, which will account for just 1 percent of the Spring Festival migration this year.

6   Authorities hope to train the Chinese to keep taking the train. The government embarked on an ambitious rail-expansion campaign, and will spend nearly $20 billion on it this year. China already has about 44,000 miles worth of railroads, a figure slated to jump to more than 60,000 miles by 2020. The system now stretches as far west as the Central Asian oasis town of Kashgar, and as high as the Tibetan plateau where construction workers have to cope with **permafrost** and high-altitude sickness in order to build the world's highest railway. The Qinghai-Tibet railroad is slated to begin operation in 2007.

7   But, until recently, the population's travel habits hadn't changed much from those days. Trains—with everyone journeying together in a communal pod, all headed in the same predetermined direction—somehow fit the central planning and collectivization of the earlier time. But rail travel now boasts some **newfangled** bells and whistles, such as the 19-mile "magnetic levitation" train that whisks you from the Pudong airport to Shanghai's city center in a matter of minutes.

> **permafrost** *n.* a layer of soil that is always frozen in countries where it is very cold 永冻层
> **newfangled** *adj.* recently designed or produced usually used to show disapproval or distrust 新玩艺儿

8   And today's Chinese are locked into a growing love affair with the automobile—a symbol of the country's blossoming sense of individuality and spontaneity. Drive north of Beijing on most weekends and you'll find the sinuous roads near the Great Wall and the Ming Tombs

clogged with Beijing families in their own cars, heading out to see the sights, go fishing or enjoy a **rustic** meal in a farmer's home. "We love to go wherever and whenever we want," says Beijing auto **buff** Wang Qishun.

9   Wang recalls that he got caught in a fierce snowstorm a few years ago after he and his family hopped into their Jeep Cherokee on the spur of the moment to drive 785 miles from Beijing to Shanghai during the Spring Festival. "It took us 17 hours to get there, at least five hours more than normal!" he laughs, claiming he had the time of his life. Wang also opened Beijing's first (and only) drive-in movie theater. Private car ownership is still prohibitively expensive for many citizens, though, so the theater sometimes lets you rent a vehicle if you show up without your own wheels.

> **rustic** *adj.* simple, old-fashioned, and not spoiled by modern developments, in a way that is typical of the countryside 乡村的
> **buff** *n.* sb who is interested in wine, films, etc. and knows a lot about them 行家，爱好者
> **bane** *n.* sth that causes trouble or makes people unhappy 祸根

10   For all the new railroads being built, China's highways are proliferating even faster. Compared to just 1,900 miles a decade ago, the mainland's expressway network already surpasses 19,000 miles, making it the second biggest in the world next to the United States, says Professor Yang. "But in the long run, keeping environmental protection in mind, we need to speed up rail construction," he says. "We need to conserve our use of energy, especially petrol." Indeed, traffic jams are the **bane** of big cities such as Beijing, and noxious vehicle emissions help make China home to four fifths of the world's most polluted cities, according to the World Bank.

11   For now, the choice between traveling by road versus rail remains dictated largely by cost. And officials clearly hope that, in the future, a sense of environmental protection and social responsibility will prevail, prompting citizens to choose trains over gas-guzzling, pollution-emitting private cars. Still, as more and more Chinese join the middle class, many members of the mainland's "me generation" will likely turn their backs on the notion of "collective travel"—and simply hit the road on their own.

(Words: 902)

• Second Reading •

Directions: Read the text again more carefully to find enough information for Exercises I, II & III.

Exercise I True or False

Directions: Please state whether the following statements are true or false (T/F) according to what you've found in the text.

1. Chinese New Year is based on the lunar calendar, and is the longest and most popular holiday of the year.
2. From Jan. 14 to Feb. 22, more than 2 billion journeys will be made by rail, road and air.
3. Zhengzhou saw a fourth day of chaos on Tuesday as stranded passengers—some of whom used nearby underground parking garages and Internet cafes as ad hoc waiting rooms—crowded around the train station.
4. The majority of travelers during Spring Festival vacation are migrant workers.
5. Chinese rail travel is cheaper and safer than traveling by car.
6. The Qinghai-Tibet railroad is slated to begin operation in 2007.
7. The 16-mile "magnetic levitation" train whisks you from the Pudong airport to Shanghai's city center in a matter of minutes.
8. Chinese citizen's growing love for the automobile symbolizes the country's blossoming sense of individuality and spontaneity.
9. Vehicle emissions make China home to four fifths of the world's most polluted cities, according to the World Bank.
10. As more and more Chinese join the middle class, many members of the mainland's "me generation" will likely adopt the notion of "collective travel".

Exercise II Word Inference

Directions: Often you can guess the meaning of a word/expression by reading the words around it. Please read the given sentence to see how each word/expression in bold type is used in the text. Then choose the answer that is closest in meaning to the bold-faced word/expression.

1. They're on the move already, armies of migrants carrying massive suitcases and cloth bundles—often balanced on shoulder poles—**bulging** with clothes, toys, electric appliances and other gifts for relatives back home. Hundreds of millions of such family

reunions are scheduled for the period from Jan. 14 to Feb. 22.
   A. contain	B. protrude
   C. combine	D. fill
2. The following day 100,000 passengers were stranded at Beijing's main railway station, and thousands of other **disgruntled** travelers packed stations in Zhengzhou and Shanghai.
   A. dissatisfied	B. troubled
   C. saddened	D. excited
3. China already has about 44,000 miles worth of railroads, a figure **slated** to jump to more than 60,000 miles by 2020.
   A. planned	B. determined
   C. decided	D. happened
4. But rail travel now boasts some newfangled bells and whistles, such as the 19-mile "magnetic levitation" train that **whisks** you from the Pudong airport to Shanghai's city center in a matter of minutes.
   A. shake	B. take
   C. mix	D. push
5. Drive north of Beijing on most weekends and you'll find the **sinuous** roads near the Great Wall and the Ming Tombs clogged with Beijing families in their own cars, heading out to see the sights, go fishing or enjoy a rustic meal in a farmer's home.
   A. spacious	B. bumpy
   C. rough	D. zigzagging
6. Drive north of Beijing on most weekends and you'll find the sinuous roads near the Great Wall and the Ming Tombs **clogged** with Beijing families in their own cars, heading out to see the sights, go fishing or enjoy a rustic meal in a farmer's home.
   A. combined	B. decorated
   C. blocked	D. paralleled
7. Private car ownership is still **prohibitively** expensive for many citizens, though, so the theater sometimes lets you rent a vehicle if you show up without your own wheels.
   A. probably	B. extremely
   C. slightly	D. invitingly
8. Indeed, traffic jams are the bane of big cities such as Beijing, and **noxious** vehicle emissions help make China home to four fifths of the world's most polluted cities, according to the World Bank.
   A. toxic	B. heavy

C. notorious   D. disgusting

9. For now, the choice between traveling by road versus rail remains **dictated** largely by cost. And officials clearly hope that, in the future, a sense of environmental protection and social responsibility will prevail, prompting citizens to choose trains over gas-guzzling, pollution-emitting private cars.

   A. say   B. tell
   C. allow   D. determine

10. For now, the choice between traveling by road versus rail remains dictated largely by cost. And officials clearly hope that, in the future, a sense of environmental protection and social responsibility will prevail, prompting citizens to choose trains over gas-**guzzling**, pollution-emitting private cars.

    A. use economically   B. use wastefully
    C. pollute heavily   D. pollute slightly

Exercise III   Discussion
Directions: Please discuss the following questions in pairs or groups.

1. What do you think of magnetic levitation train?
2. What is your experience of traveling during the season of Spring Festival?

Text B

China 2.0
By Melinda Liu

Warming-up Exercises

☞ What changes has your family undergone in recent years?
☞ Do you like the changes in your community? Why or why not?

74

• First reading •

Directions: Now please read the following passage as fast as you can and summarize the main idea.

1   ___A___, but also to how many times they say it. This month President Hu Jintao has embraced a new **mantra**, stressing "sustainable development," "innovation" and "a resource-saving, environment-friendly society." He uttered those buzzwords in his New Year's address, then at a high-profile science and technology conference, and then again last week during an inspection tour of Fujian province. In a significant departure from his predecessors' focus on **no-holds-barred** GDP growth, Hu is calling for nothing less than a quantum shift in China's economic-development model, deeming it "an important and urgent strategic task."

2   China has already achieved a quarter century of unprecedented economic growth. Now Beijing is essentially saying that it needs to keep growing in a more responsible way, emphasizing environmental protection, more energy efficiency and cutting-edge technology. Software **mavens** might call this new vision China 2.0. You don't have to be a rocket scientist (or a Politburo member) to see that the mainland's winning formula of cheap labor, heavy investment and nearly double-digit GDP growth can't last forever. Without a fresh **paradigm**, authorities believe, China will increasingly suffer from environmental degradation, destabilizing income disparity and social unrest. The question is whether the country can afford to shift gears now—or whether such concerns could cost it the competitive advantages that have made China's economy the most-talked-about in the world today.

3   ___B___. According to the World Bank, pollution and other environmental damage may be costing the Chinese economy between 8 and 12 percent of GDP annually, due to medical-care expenses and damage to crops and marine products. The mainland is now home to 16 of the world's 20 most polluted cities.

> **mantra** n. a word or sound that is repeated as a prayer or to help people meditate （宗）颂歌
> **no-holds-barred** adj. (only before noun) a no-holds-barred discussion, situation, etc. is one in which there are no rules or limits 无限制的
> **maven** n. (AmE) someone who knows a lot about a particular subject 行家
> **paradigm** n. (technical) a model or example that shows how something works or is produced 范式，模范

More than three fifths of the country's rivers and lakes are tainted with chemicals, industrial waste or toxic spills like the recent Songhua River benzene slick, which contaminated the water supply in the city of Harbin for days.

4 Already scarce arable land is disappearing as rapacious real-estate developers gobble up farmland. Though China is desperate for energy, the country uses power inefficiently. Experts estimate that the country uses three times as much energy per unit of GDP as the United States, and nine times more than Japan. Meanwhile, rural discontent has flared over land seizures, pollution and lagging wages—roughly one third of what urban workers make. Last week the Public Security Ministry admitted that incidents of social unrest grew by more than 6 percent in 2005. "Ordinary people aren't satisfied with the results of fast economic growth," says economics professor Xia Yeliang of Tsinghua University, __C__.

5 Chinese leaders are essentially admitting that brains, not brawn, are the key to what Hu calls an "innovation-based economy." The concept is an echo of U.S. economist Paul Krugman's 1990s critique of East Asia's export-based economies, in which he touted the benefits of "inspiration" rather than "perspiration." Chinese experts have even revealed when they believe this paradigm shift should occur—when a country's per capita GDP reaches the $1,000 to $3,000 range. (China's per capita GDP exceeded the $1,000 threshold in 2003.)

6 Certainly, __D__, which will hasten the country's move up the development food chain—and away from the "embarrassing" situation of having to export 800 million shirts to pay for a single imported airplane, as one domestic newspaper recently put it. "China should not be the factory of the world any longer," says Yang Fan, a professor of commerce at the China Politics and Law University. Economic liberals have been shouting for more innovation for years, even decades, says Yang. The difference is that "this time, I think the government is taking our suggestions."

7 As part of his call last week to create an "innovation economy" within 15 years, Hu urged the Chinese to invent **proprietary** technologies and vowed to boost state R&D spending, which was just 1.23 percent of GDP in 2004. (Japan and the United States spend 3.3 percent and 2.7 percent of GDP, respectively, according to the OECD.) China is already cracking down on construction projects that fail to conduct required environmental feasibility studies. Beijing is pursuing clean-energy sources; to maintain high GDP growth rates, China needs to double its power-generation capacity by 2020.

> **proprietary** *adj.* being used, produced, or marketed under exclusive legal right of the inventor or maker; specifically: a drug (as a patent medicine) that is protected by secrecy, patent, or copyright against free competition as to name, product, composition, or process of manufacture 受专利保护的

8   Beijing plans to spend $185 billion by 2020 to develop renewable energy. In particular, the Chinese need to be weaned off coal, a cheap but dirty energy source that accounts for more than 70 percent of the country's power production. Although energy conservation and recycling are two other trendy catchphrases nowadays, many Chinese remain hugely wasteful. Leaky faucets are left to run, partly because urban water is only about one tenth as expensive as in Germany. Petrol is heavily subsidized, costing about one fourth of what it does in the United States. Although they've raised water fees incrementally, Chinese authorities worry that substantial water, power and fuel price hikes will prompt protests. "To realize 'green GDP,' one has to pay a big price," says analyst Li Shi of the Chinese Academy of Social Sciences.

9   ___E___ will be a long-term challenge. And many provincial governments may resist. "Local government officials won't be happy with this idea," says Xia. "They might support it [publicly], but boycott it behind the scenes." Local authorities chase quantifiable achievements that come with making and building things. Most serve three-to five-year terms in office, explains Xia, so they want to see the kind of tangible results that lead to promotions—more factories, rising exports. Dong Baoping, dean of the Beijing Science and Technology Management College, says that local governments have often "turned a deaf ear to the notion of environmental protection."

> **trade-off** *n.* a balance between two opposing things, that you are willing to accept in order to achieve something 权衡，协调
> **sizzling** *adj.* (*esp AmE*) very hot 很热的

10   There are no easy answers. Li says that Beijing may have to choose between "slower economic growth with high quality, or rapid economic growth with low quality." That's an unappealing **trade-off** in a nation that must generate at least 17 million new jobs every year for young people entering the work force. In other words, China cannot afford to let traditional GDP growth dip too low. "We have a serious employment situation; we need to balance feeding people adequately while doing a good job of environmental protection," says Li. To succeed at that task, Hu and his Politburo colleagues may well be hoping for a second economic miracle.

(Words: 1076)

• Second Reading •

Directions: Read the text again more carefully to find enough information for Exercises I, II, III & IV.

Exercise I Understanding Text Organization

Directions: You may find there are a few sentences (segments) missing from the passage. Read the article through and decide where the following sentences should go.

1. Certainly China is already paying a heavy price for its economic success

2. China has become almost obsessed with technological innovation

3. Turning China's behemoth economy in a different direction

4. "so the government has embraced the idea of 'green GDP'"

5. If you're a China watcher, you don't just listen to what top Beijing leaders say

Exercise II Multiple-Choice Questions

Directions: Please choose the best answer to the following questions.

1. When did President Hu first embrace the new mantra, stressing sustainable development, innovation, etc.?

    A. in his New Year's address

    B. at a science and technology conference

    C. during an inspection tour of Fujian province.

    D. at a meeting with his Politburo colleagues

2. What does China's new economic model emphasize?

    A. environmental protection

    B. more energy efficiency

    C. cutting-edge technology

    D. all of the above

3. According to the World Bank, pollution and other environmental damage may be costing the Chinese economy between 8 and 12 percent of GDP annually. Why?

    A. Because of medical-care expenses.

    B. Because of medical-care expenses and damage to crops.

    C. Because of medical-care expenses and damage to marine products.

    D. Because of medical-care expenses and damage to crops and marine products.

4. Where does rural discontent come from in China according to the author?

   A. Land seizures and pollution.

   B. Land seizures and lagging wages.

   C. Land seizures, pollution and lagging wages.

   D. Lagging wages—roughly one third of what urban workers make.

5. Which country is not mentioned in this article?

   A. The United States.

   B. Singapore.

   C. Germany.

   D. Japan.

Exercise III Word Inference

Directions: Often you can guess the meaning of a word/expression by reading the words around it. Please read the given sentence to see how each word/expression in bold type is used in the text. Then choose the answer that is closest in meaning to the bold-faced word/expression.

1. He uttered those **buzzwords** in his New Year's address, then at a high-profile science and technology conference, and then again last week during an inspection tour of Fujian province.

   A. saying   B. crossword

   C. catchphrase   D. motto

2. Now Beijing is essentially saying that it needs to keep growing in a more responsible way, emphasizing environmental protection, more energy efficiency and **cutting-edge** technology.

   A. newest   B. strangest

   C. oldest   D. most usual

3. More than three fifths of the country's rivers and lakes are **tainted** with chemicals, industrial waste or toxic spills like the recent Songhua River benzene slick, which contaminated the water supply in the city of Harbin for days.

   A. pollute   B. paint

   C. tarnish   D. color

4. Already scarce arable land is disappearing as **rapacious** real-estate developers gobble up farmland.
   A. rich   B. crazy
   C. greedy   D. rude

5. Chinese leaders are essentially admitting that brains, not **brawn**, are the key to what Hu calls an "innovation-based economy."
   A. intellectual ability   B. spiritual value
   C. mental situation   D. physical strength

6. The concept is an echo of U.S. economist Paul Krugman's 1990s critique of East Asia's export-based economies, in which he **touted** the benefits of "inspiration" rather than "perspiration."
   A. criticize   B. blame
   C. propose   D. advocate

7. Although they've raised water fees **incrementally**, Chinese authorities worry that substantial water, power and fuel price hikes will prompt protests.
   A. gradually   B. sharply
   C. slightly   D. greatly

8. Although they've raised water fees incrementally, Chinese authorities worry that substantial water, power and fuel price **hikes** will prompt protests.
   A. walk   B. rise
   C. flux   D. change

9. "They might support it [publicly], but **boycott** it behind the scenes."
   A. refuse   B. destroy
   C. criticize   D. resist

10. That's an **unappealing** trade-off in a nation that must generate at least 17 million new jobs every year for young people entering the work force. In other words, China cannot afford to let traditional GDP growth dip too low.
    A. unsurprising   B. unimportant
    C. unpleasant   D. unusual

Exercise IV   Discussion

Directions: Please discuss the following questions in pairs or groups.

1. What obstacles might Beijing be faced with in shifting to a new economic model?
2. What does "software mavens might call this new vision China 2.0" in paragraph 2 line 3 mean?
3. Does the author have an attitude in this article? Give evidence to support your stance.

Text C

China Juggles Tombs and Dragon Boats

By Keith Bradsher

1   HONG KONG, Nov. 9 — A Chinese government panel announced plans on Friday to revamp the holiday schedule to re-emphasize traditional festivals at the expense of the Marxist May Day celebration.

2   The new schedule aims to address the severe overloading of China's air, rail and road links in the first week of May, when virtually the entire country goes on vacation. But gridlock may remain around the two other major holidays—essentially a week each— at the Chinese New Year and in the first week of October.

3   Government officials, laborers and executives alike try to visit distant family members or vacation destinations during those holidays, frequently producing transportation nightmares.

4   The panel's plans were posted on the Internet for public comment on Friday and in theory could still be changed. But the official Xinhua news agency said the plan was ready to go into place early next year, suggesting that all relevant government agencies had reached a consensus that is unlikely to be altered.

5   The plan calls for trimming the May 1 holiday to one working day from three. At the same time, three traditional Chinese festivals will each become one-day public holidays.

6   The new holidays are Tomb-Sweeping Day in April, the Dragon Boat Festival in June and the Mid-Autumn Festival in September. The dates of the festivals vary on Western calendars, because they are determined by a lunar calendar.

7   Chinese New Year, usually in late January or early February, and National Day, Oct. 1, will continue as three-day national holidays. They typically expand to seven days through the rearrangement of weekends: if the official holidays fall on Monday, Tuesday and Wednesday, for example, then Thursday and Friday frequently become holidays as well, while the

following Saturday and Sunday become workdays.

8   Under the new schedule, the first official day of Chinese New Year will also be recalculated to fall one day earlier, making it easier for laborers facing cross-country bus and train rides to reach their families in time for the height of the celebrations.

9   James Thompson, the chairman of Crown Worldwide Holdings, a major Asian moving company based in Hong Kong, said the current practice of taking nearly weeklong holidays posed severe problems for his industry.

10   "We actually have to tell our overseas offices to avoid shipping into China during that period," he said. "Everything is shut."

11   In many rural areas, tombs are once more decorated with flowers and other tributes on Tomb-Sweeping Day, even though China discourages burials in favor of cremation. The ban on burials, enforced particularly in or near cities, is intended to conserve land and prevent the reappearance of lavish burial ceremonies that sometimes bankrupted even affluent families.

(Words: 500)

Exercise I Discussion

Directions: Please discuss the following questions in pairs or groups.

1. What is the change in China's holiday schedule?

2. What is your attitude towards the change and why?
3. Do you agree with the author's attitude? Use examples to comment.

Exercise II Writing

Directions: The articles in this unit are related to the Chinese society. Write a composition about what you think we can do to make China's progress more sustainable in about 200 words.

UNIT SIX

CULTURAL DIFFERENCE

Target of the Unit

☞ To get a glimpse of the cultural gaps among nations in various aspects
☞ To practice reading skills
☞ To enlarge your vocabulary

1) LEAD IN

Directions: In this unit, you will read 3 passages about differences between countries or nations; these differences are manifested in many ways; while you read you can focus on these differences and reflect upon them.

2) DISCUSSION

What do you think are the differences that bring countries or nations apart? And conversely what are the common points between countries that bring them together?

Text A

China, U.S. Taking Notes on Education

By Mitchell Landsberg

Warming-up Exercises

☞ What do you know about China's education system in general and higher education in particular?
☞ What do you know about America's education system?

• First reading •

Directions: Now please read the following passage as fast as you can and summarize the main idea.

1   Light snow **speckled** the bare dirt courtyard outside teacher Cai Limei's fifth-grade classroom. Inside, an ancient radiator was barely warm to the touch.

2   The classroom at the Gaoyakou Central Primary School, about an hour outside Beijing and not far from the Great Wall, was as austere as it was cold. Little more than a Chinese flag and a blackboard served for ornamentation. Yet the students, bundled in colorful **parkas** and scarves, were bubbling excitedly as they sat in **knots** of twos and threes, trying to come up with answers to a series of grammar exercises.

3   An American teacher walking into this room might be put off by the lack of creature comforts, but surely would recognize the teaching methods being deployed by Cai, an enthusiastic 27-year-old in a puffy, **shin**-length blue coat.

4   And with good reason. Although she teaches at a school that outwardly appears little changed from the old days, Cai is on the cutting edge of Chinese educational reform, using methods based on those used in the United States.

5   "In my time as a student," she said, "we accepted only what we were taught." Now, as a teacher, she tries to encourage "more active thinking," letting students figure out answers for themselves.

6   "It's better now," she said.

> **speckle** v. to cover with small marks or spots 带有斑点
> **parka** n. a thick warm jacket with a hood 带风帽的外套
> **knot** n. a small group of people standing close together 群，簇
> **shin** n. the front part of your leg between your knee and your foot 胫部

The Best of Both Worlds

7   In many ways, China and the United States represent the *yin* and *yang* of international education. Whereas China's top-down system places supreme emphasis on tightly structured, disciplined learning, the United States has a highly decentralized system that places greater importance on

critical thinking and "student-centered" learning.

8   Still, in recent years, the Chinese and American systems have been taking baby steps toward each other, learning and adapting what the other does best.

9   American educators have been exploring why Chinese and other Asian students do so well in math and science, and trying to apply some of their findings to U.S. classrooms.

10   The Chinese, in turn, are trying to distill the American genius for innovation, recognizing that, for all its faults, the U.S. educational system is unrivaled at turning out creative minds—inventors, filmmakers, rock 'n' roll stars and Nobel laureates among them.

11   "The two systems cannot totally merge," said Zhou Mansheng, who studies the American educational system in his role as deputy director of China's National Center for Educational Development Research. "What they can do is have a very deep understanding of each other's educational systems and try to learn from them."

Math, the Chinese Way

12   Thousands of American educators have visited China in recent years, meeting with education officials and shuttling to showcase schools selected by the government. These trips have led to changes in some American schools and a general consensus among education leaders that more change is needed, especially in the teaching of math.

13   At the root of the difference is the idea, in Chinese and other East Asian math curricula, "that there is a very small body of factual mathematics that students need to learn, but they need to learn it really, really well," said R. James Milgram, professor emeritus of mathematics at Stanford University and one of the authors of California's public school math standards.

14   Last fall, the National Council of Teachers of Mathematics adopted a policy that urges American schools to focus math studies on just three basic topics in each grade from pre-kindergarten through eighth. That idea, Milgram said, comes from Asian curricula. However, he said, American schools will have a difficult time emulating their Asian counterparts unless they sharply improve the math abilities of primary school teachers.

15   China has a powerful, millenniums-old tradition of education that is woven deep into its societal DNA. But just as that can't be bottled and shipped, neither is it easy for a society such as China's to mine the best of the American educational tradition.

16   That hasn't stopped it from trying.

17   Under the leadership of Zhou and his colleagues, China's educational system has been undergoing a major overhaul since 1999, when the government recognized that the country's explosive economic growth could not be sustained without a better-educated workforce. It set out to improve the educational system from bottom to top—upgrading rural schools,

quintupling the size of its university system and, perhaps most radically, bringing more critical thinking and creativity into its classrooms.

18   China wants to become a big nation of innovation in the 21st century," Zhou said in an interview in Beijing. "To meet this objective, China wants to cultivate more creative talent."

19   To do this, the Education Ministry has revamped the national curriculum and begun training teachers in a more interactive style. There will be less rote learning, more give-and-take with teachers, and more exercises such as the one at the Gaoyakou Central Primary School, where the students learn in groups.

20   "This is very difficult for them to do," said Vivian Stewart, vice president for education at the Asia Society, a New York-based organization that promotes U.S. relations with Asia. "Given the class sizes that they have"—Chinese schools often have 50 or 60 students per class—"it's very difficult to think about doing a lot of projects and discussion-oriented **pedagogy**."

21   "It's a very organized society, and when they set their mind to go in a particular direction, they are able to drive things in that direction," Stewart said.

New Textbooks for Old

22   The change is coming slowly to the Changping No. 2 Middle School. This high school is considered one of the best in the nation. The school, on an attractive, well-equipped campus in a modern, if heavily polluted, suburb of Beijing, it has 450 students, more than 95% of whom are expected to go to college.

23   Administrators and teachers say they are committed to reforming their curriculum, but they are clearly in no hurry. New textbooks are scheduled to arrive next year; in the meantime, "we are in the middle of changing from the old way to the new way," said Vice Principal Sun Li.

24   The difference is not immediately noticeable in classes, where students tend to sit in traditional-style rows of desks and listen to lectures. Math teacher Yang Guihong, a tall, willowy woman, said she had changed her teaching to make it "more practical," more connected to everyday life.

> **pedagogy** *n.* the art or method of teaching; pedagogics 教学，教学法
> **trigonometry** *n.* the part of mathematics concerned with the relationship between the angles and sides of triangles 三角学

25   "The point is, we make the students curious first," she explained through an interpreter, "then we tell them what to do."

26   By most measures, her students are well ahead of their U.S. counterparts. Her first-year students—the equivalent of American 10th-graders—are studying **trigonometry** and set theory; her second-year students have moved on to linear programming, among other

concepts.

27   Down the hall, students in Wang Yu's English class are listening to the teacher read from a textbook, and reciting translations about, among other things, American high school dropouts.

28   "Most high school students," Wang reads, "drop out of school because a) they have failing grades b) they take no interest in classes c) they are discriminated against d) they are lazy and not intelligent."

29   The correct answer, he says, is B.

30   Outside class, several students say that despite having taken English classes since third grade, they can't speak the language — the result, they say, of an educational system that is aimed primarily at preparing them for college entrance exams.

31   "There's too much focus on the grammar and very little on actual communication," said Yang Huan, 17, speaking through an interpreter.

32   The students agree that they have seen scant signs of reform.

33   "I feel like a lot of what we learn is not practical, and not usable after we graduate," said Pei Pei, 16, a tall, thin girl with glasses.

34   The Gaoyakou school sits at the bottom of an imposing hill in the modest farming village of Wayao.

35   The slightly ramshackle school buildings and plain classrooms are a far cry from those at Changping. They bear little evidence that the calendar has flipped much past the 1970s. Whereas nearly all the students at Changping are expected to go to college, roughly a third of the students in Wayao are expected to drop out before high school.

36   But perhaps because they have less to lose, the mostly young staff at the Gaoyakou school has embraced the new curriculum with enthusiasm. Zhang Shuhong, a 31-year-old who is the equivalent of a vice principal, said the school adopted new textbooks and a new curriculum in 2004. Many of the teachers are fresh out of college, where they learned the new teaching methods, and needed no prodding to employ them.

37   "I think it's better than before," Zhang said. "It's more adaptable to students' development."

38   The new way, he said, "encourages students' open thinking…. Before, we just made kids memorize things. Now, they memorize less and think more."

(Words:1482)

Second Reading

Directions: Read the text again more carefully to find enough information for Exercises I, II & III.

Exercise I True or False

Directions: Please state whether the following statements are true or false (T/F) according to what you've found in the text.

1. The classroom at the Gaoyakou Central Primary School was outside Beijing and not far from the Great Wall.
2. An American teacher might be put off by the lack of creature comforts in the school.
3. China's top-down system places supreme emphasis on tightly structured, disciplined learning.
4. The United States has a highly centralized system that places greater importance on critical thinking and "student-centered" learning.
5. The Chinese educational systems cannot merge with the American educational system.
6. China's Education Ministry has revamped the national curriculum and begun training teachers in a more interactive style.
7. Changping No. 2 Middle School is on an attractive, well-equipped campus in a modern suburb of Beijing.
8. Changping No. 2 Middle School is quick in its curriculum reform.
9. The staff of the Gaoyakou Central Primary School embraced the new curriculum with enthusiasm.
10. The National Council of Teachers of Mathematics adopted a policy that urges American schools to focus math studies on just three basic topics in each grade from pre-kindergarten through eighth.

Exercise II Word Inference

Directions: Often you can guess the meaning of a word/expression by reading the words around it. Please read the given sentence to see how each word/expression in bold type is used in the text. Then choose the answer that is closest in meaning to the bold-faced word/expression.

1. The classroom at the Gaoyakou Central Primary School, about an hour outside Beijing and not far from the Great Wall, was as **austere** as it was cold. Little more than a Chinese flag and a blackboard served for ornamentation.

    A. strict   B. serious
    C. simple   D. shiny

2. An American teacher walking into this room might be put off by the lack of creature comforts, but surely would recognize the teaching methods being **deployed** by Cai, an enthusiastic 27-year-old in a puffy, shin-length blue coat.

    A. employ   B. enhance
    C. adapt   D. decide

3. The Chinese, in turn, are trying to **distill** the American genius for innovation, recognizing that, for all its faults, the U.S. educational system is unrivaled at turning out creative minds—inventors, filmmakers, rock 'n' roll stars and Nobel laureates among them.

    A. purify   B. remove
    C. obtain   D. dig

4. The Chinese, in turn, are trying to distill the American genius for innovation, recognizing that, for all its faults, the U.S. educational system is **unrivaled** at turning out creative minds—inventors, filmmakers, rock 'n' roll stars and Nobel laureates among them.

    A. best   B. great
    C. bad   D. worst

5. That idea, Milgram said, comes from Asian curricula. However, he said, American schools will have a difficult time **emulating** their Asian counterparts unless they sharply improve the math abilities of primary school teachers.

    A. migrate   B. imitate
    C. train   D. guard

6. But just as that can't be bottled and shipped, neither is it easy for a society such China's to **mine** the best of the American educational tradition.

    A. get   B. dig
    C. hide   D. learn

7. Under the leadership of Zhou and his colleagues, China's educational system has been undergoing a major **overhaul** since 1999, when the government recognized that the country's explosive economic growth could not be sustained without a better-educated workforce.

    A. pull   B. change

C. move D. process
8. To do this, the Education Ministry has **revamped** the national curriculum and begun training teachers in a more interactive style.
   A. change B. study
   C. check D. supervise
9. The Gaoyakou school sits at the bottom of an **imposing** hill in the modest farming village of Wayao.
   A. dirty B. grey
   C. dark D. large
10. The slightly **ramshackle** school buildings and plain classrooms are a far cry from those at Changping.
    A. exciting B. similar
    C. better D. tumbledown

Exercise III Discussion

Directions: Please discuss the following questions in pairs or groups.

1. Do you or your friends have any experience of study in America? What strikes you most?
2. Are you satisfied with the current curriculum on your campus?

Text B

Ambassador Bridge Controversy Highlights Cultural Divide

By Dante Chinni

Warming-up Exercises

☞ What do you know about the differences between Canada and the United States?

☞ Despite the cultural differences between the two countries, what are the vital elements that make these two countries coexist peacefully without rifts for so long?

• **First reading** •

Directions: Now please read the following passage as fast as you can and summarize the main idea.

1   In sheer physical terms, the Ambassador Bridge is everything a bridge should be. It connects two pieces of land—the United States and Canada. It traverses water—the Detroit River. It even has a certain **grandeur** as an international crossing and an "ambassador" for the two countries. And while the twin 386-foot steel towers may lack the beauty of the Golden Gate, the "Motor City" isn't exactly San Francisco, either.

> **grandeur** *n.* impressive beauty, power, or size
> 宏伟，壮观

2   ___A___. In many ways, the Ambassador only emphasizes the sibling rivalry of the US and Canada. In population and in skyline, Detroit dwarfs Windsor, the Canadian burg across the water. When Windsor built a casino to boost tax revenues, Detroit built three of its own.

3   And the Ambassador itself, since its completion in 1929, represents the cultural differences between the two cities. It isn't jointly owned by the US and Canadian governments; it isn't even owned by the US alone. In a salute to America's love of capitalism

and the individual, it is owned by a single citizen, Detroit-area businessman Manuel "Matty" Moroun. And that's where the differences deepen, because Mr. Moroun wants to build a new bridge alongside the existing one.

4   Another bridge full of commerce? says the Motor City. Why not?

5   Another bridge full of traffic? says Windsor. No, thank you.

6   Whoever wins, someone is going to get mad.

7   __B__. The Ambassador is the busiest commercial crossing in North America and is a crucial link for the local auto industry. More than a quarter of all trade between the US and Canada flows over the bridge or through the Windsor Tunnel—an estimated $1 billion daily. Heightened security since 2001 has hobbled the movement of commerce and traffic, which is estimated to grow 57 percent and 127 percent, respectively, in the next 30 years.

8   But where, oh where, to build? Detroit wants the next thoroughfare to come through the city. Windsor wants it anywhere but in its own backyard. And that difference highlights the cultural dissimilarities of these two cities and countries.

9   When is a bridge not a bridge? Maybe when it highlights a divide. It's not that the cities themselves are so utterly different. Detroit, like Buffalo, N.Y., home of another big border crossing, is one of the more Canadian American cities.

10 Unlike other Americans, many Detroiters can hum the tune for the Canadian Broadcasting Corporation's legendary TV show "Hockey Night." __C__ and has a restaurant devoted to its hockey **franchise**, the Red Wings. Tim Horton's, the ubiquitous Canadian doughnut chain, has a **beachhead** in greater Detroit and can often be spotted across the street from metro-area Dunkin' Donuts. And both cities understand the pain of long, gray winters.

11 But the contrasts have always been there—some subtle, some more obvious.

12 Cross from Detroit to Windsor, for example, and **voilà**, McDonald's offers vinegar with its French fries. The money features birds and bears and colorful scenes of children on skates; one- and two-dollar denominations come in coins. "Center" becomes "centre." And radio station call letters all begin with K rather than W.

13 Drive the streets in the two cities and the faces are different: More than

> **franchise** *n.* a permission given by a company to someone who wants to sell its goods or services 特许权
> **beachhead** *n.* an area of shore that has been taken from an enemy by force, and from which the army can prepare to attack a country（部队登陆后准备进攻时所建的）滩头阵地
> **voilà** *interj.* (*French*) used when you are showing or telling someone something surprising 瞧（表示惊讶或满意之感叹词）

82 percent of Detroit's residents are African-American, while only 3 percent of Windsorites are black.

14 ___D___.

15 On the Canadian side, the bridge descends like a spaceship, dropping down out of nowhere on the houses and streets that surround the University of Windsor. Single-family homes, some of them makeshift student housing, fill the side streets, while shops, restaurants, and clubs line Wyandotte Street, one of the town's main drags.

16 In "The Bookroom," a small used-book store, owner Ann Beer shakes her head when she talks about the bridge. "The problem is, wherever they put it here, it really will mess up part of Windsor," she says. "I think it should go way down east somewhere. Far from here." On the wall, Beer has posted a simple sign: "Did you know that 50% of the trucks coming through the Ambassador Bridge just take a short-cut through Canada."

17 Nearby at the University Barber Shop, proprietor Adolfo Macera shares Beer's concerns, if not her resolve: "Wherever they put the next span, they should put it out of here. It's too much."

18 "But that's the big boys over there," he continues, referring to Moroun, the mayor, and the city.

19 Indeed, freshly poured foundations for a new bridge span are already sitting beside the overpass—though Windsor has passed a one-year **moratorium** on building or demolition in the area until a community-improvement plan is developed.

20 Of course, the view from Motor City is slightly different. "We don't care [where that bridge goes], as long as it goes through Detroit," says James Canning, spokesman for Detroit Mayor Kwame Kilpatrick. ___E___.

21 The riverfront wasn't always the place to be: For decades, Detroit treated that prime real estate as a ghetto for warehouses and cement silos. In the past 10 years, however, the city has pumped tens of millions into new parks and a riverwalk to lure people back. Yet those plans do not extend all the way down to the Ambassador, where land is devoted to transit and cargo, warehouses and train tracks, and cries of "don't let the 401 run through Windsor" earn no more than a shrug.

> **moratorium** *n.* an official stopping of an activity for a period of time 暂停，终止

22 Mexicantown, a commercial and entertainment area based on Bagley Street, filled with three and four-story buildings, is by no means pro-Ambassador addition. There are grumbles here that Moroun hasn't come through with investments he's promised, and doubts as to the

integrity of the bridge-planning process.

23 "This is all about the mayor and Moroun," says Jeanette Avila in an exasperated voice. "Who knows what deal they have worked out?" Ms. Avila, a member of the Mexicantown board of directors and owner of El Rancho Mexican Restaurant, suspects Moroun will get his way.

24 Even so, the bridge isn't considered the community killer it is across the river. In fact, some here have embraced it. Just this Cinco de Mayo, the Michigan International Welcome Center and Mexican Mercado opened as an $18 million jointly funded private-public venture: 45,000 square feet of retail space, a public market, and a plaza. Roads and sidewalks are being **reconfigured**; a fancy pedestrian bridge will cross the highways. The area, according to artists' conceptions, is on its way to becoming a combination park and entertainment district. In decidedly un-Winsdsorian fashion, it aims to draw people across the bridge.

> **reconfigure** *v.* to rearrange the elements or settings of 重新安排，重新规划

25 So even as many in Mexicantown officially oppose a second span of the Ambassador, others say it wouldn't be all bad—and would likely bring more people to explore, shop, and dine.

26 Oh, yes, and to leave a few more of those colorful Canadian dollars when they leave.

(Words: 1180)

• Second Reading •

Directions: Read the text again more carefully to find enough information for Exercises I, II, III & IV.

Exercise I   Understanding Text Organization

Directions: You may find there are a few sentences (segments) missing from the passage. Read the article through and decide where the following sentences should go.

1. No one really questions the need for another bridge
2. Looking at where the Ambassador Bridge touches down in each city only brings the

differences into sharper relief

3. The city even likes to call itself "Hockeytown"

4. "We just feel that the riverfront is the place to be, and we don't see why the next bridge shouldn't be there, too"

5. In metaphorical bridge terms, however—connecting, linking, joining disparate things—the Ambassador Bridge is no bridge at all

Exercise II   Multiple-Choice Questions

Directions: Please choose the best answer to the following questions.

1. When was the Ambassador Bridge completed?
   A. 1929. B. 2001.
   C. 1928. D. 1930.

2. Who owns the Ambassador Bridge?
   A. The United States. B. Canada.
   C. The United States and Canada. D. A single citizen.

3. Which statement about Detroit and Windsor is not correct?
   A. When Windsor built a casino to boost tax revenues, Detroit built three of its own.
   B. Detroit wants the next thoroughfare to come through the city. Windsor wants it anywhere but in its own backyard.
   C. Cross from Detroit to Windsor, for example, and voilà, McDonald's offers vinegar with its French fries.
   D. More than 82 percent of Windsorites residents are African-American, while only 3 percent of Detroit's are black.

4. The busiest commercial crossing in North America is _____.
   A. Detroit B. Windsor
   C. the Ambassador Bridge D. Buffalo

5. Who is Detroit Mayor?
   A. Jeanette Avila. B. Adolfo Macera.
   C. James Canning. D. Kwame Kilpatrick.

Exercise III Word Inference

Directions: Often you can guess the meaning of a word/expression by reading the words around it. Please read the given sentence to see how each word/expression in bold type is used in the text. Then choose the answer that is closest in meaning to the bold-faced word/expression.

1. It **traverses** water—the Detroit River.
   A. tread   B. ride
   C. cross   D. hike

2. In metaphorical bridge terms, however—connecting, linking, joining **disparate** things—the Ambassador Bridge is no bridge at all.
   A. separate   B. different
   C. similar   D. integrated

3. Heightened security since 2001 has **hobbled** the movement of commerce and traffic, which is estimated to grow 57 percent and 127 percent, respectively, in the next 30 years.
   A. develop   B. impede
   C. promote   D. trigger

4. Tim Horton's, the **ubiquitous** Canadian doughnut chain, has a beachhead in greater Detroit and can often be spotted across the street from metro-area Dunkin' Donuts.
   A. pervasive   B. permanent
   C. prevailing   D. prevalent

5. Single-family homes, some of them **makeshift** student housing, fill the side streets, while shops, restaurants, and clubs line Wyandotte Street, one of the town's main drags.
   A. stopgap   B. showup
   C. makeup   D. uplift

6. Single-family homes, some of them makeshift student housing, fill the side streets, while shops, restaurants, and clubs line Wyandotte Street, one of the town's main **drags**.
   A. market   B. thoroughfare
   C. fortress   D. port

7. Indeed, freshly poured foundations for a new bridge span are already sitting beside the overpass—though Windsor has passed a one-year moratorium on building or

demolition in the area until a community-improvement plan is developed.

    A. decoration   B. construction

    C. destruction   D. repair

8. Yet those plans do not extend all the way down to the Ambassador, where land is devoted to **transit** and cargo, warehouses and train tracks, and cries of "don't let the 401 run through Windsor" earn no more than a shrug.

    A. commerce   B. transport

    C. trade   D. exchange

9. There are **grumbles** here that Moroun hasn't come through with investments he's promised, and doubts as to the integrity of the bridge-planning process.

    A. complaint   B. criticism

    C. voice   D. praise

10. "This is all about the mayor and Moroun," says Jeanette Avila in an **exasperated** voice.

    A. annoyed   B. excited

    C. surprised   D. moved

Exercise IV   Discussion

Directions: Please discuss the following questions in pairs or groups.

1. What is the relationship between Windsor and Detroit?
2. Generalize the opinions about a second span of the Ambassador Bridge in the article.

Text C

Love in a Cold and Wet Climate

By Unnamed Author

1.   Couples from mixed backgrounds living in Ireland tell Arsheen Qasim about the benefits and challenges their differing nationality, culture and religion bring to their relationships

2   Being a dark-haired, dark-eyed, petite Filipino, Cristina Cinco immediately caught Nick's eye. "It was extreme attraction at first sight," says Nick Taaffe, a 23-year-old Dubliner who met Cristina while working on a cruise boat in Canada. Cristina was the only girl on the job, and when their boss realised they were in love he moved her to another boat. So Nick decided to quit his job in defiance.

3   Cristina and Nick's summer romance was still going strong two-and-a-half years on. "We thought it couldn't go anywhere because we were from different countries and we had college. I had never thought that I would ever go visit his country." But love tugged at their hearts and Cristina came over from Canada to see Nick that Christmas. Soon after they both finished their studies she decided to move to Ireland.

4   Joana Medeiros (23) from Portugal also moved to Ireland just to be close to her Irish boyfriend of six years, Eoin O'Faolain. "I never even thought of Ireland before—I wanted to go to Japan! But I speak English and I have more opportunities here," says Joana.

5   Ireland seemed like the perfect place to meet and fall in love for medical students, Hana (22) and Eric (25). Irish-born Hana moved to Bahrain with her English mother and Indian father when she was young. She came back to study medicine at the Royal College of Surgeons in Ireland. While in her second year she met Eric, who had moved here from Connecticut.

6   "We're in this small class, and we decided to go to a comedy club just for a laugh," recalls Hana. "I arrived at his door, ready to go. I said, 'who's going as well?' He's like, 'oh, it just turned out to be you and me,' and there you go," she smiles.

7   Mauritian-Indian Minakshi (Min) Ramphul (23) met David O'Connell from Limerick in their first year studying medicine in Trinity College Dublin. They've been together for more than three years.

8   So what is it that attracts young people from different countries, cultures and religious persuasions to each other? "I found Min interesting because of the different culture. I didn't know much about Indian culture or Indian clothes or food or anything beforehand," says David.

9   IT WAS SOMETHING similar that sparked Cristina's interest in Nick. "I think Nick and I were very exciting for each other. I loved his accent, his really white skin—all the white boys in Canada are tanned!"

10   Nick confesses he knew little about Filipino culture before he met Cristina. "She

introduced me to a lot of things. Even the Filipino food was different; they didn't eat potatoes—all they eat is rice." Cristina adds, "He didn't know what sushi was, he didn't know what a mango was."

11   These young people feel that their worlds have expanded through dating a person from a different background to theirs. Learning cultural lessons becomes part of the daily routine. Joana's social life didn't revolve around drinking alcohol. "I'm trying to cut down," says Eoin. "Living in Portugal, it was nice to know you can have a good time with people without relying on alcohol. It's just great to get a different viewpoint because we Irish are kind of stuck in a certain attitude."

12   Despite the excitement of being exposed to new cultures, most of these young people in Ireland feel that being in an intercultural relationship is not that different from being in a relationship with someone from the same race or country.

13   "I come from Mauritius and it's multicultural, it's very mixed, and mixed relationships there are quite common, so it wasn't strange for me," explains Min.

14   Hana comes from a similar cosmopolitan background. "Bahrain's a really multi-cultural, liberal society compared with Saudi. Bahrain is essentially the same as over here, so it was fairly relaxed growing up and I went to an English school."

15   But what do the more conservative parents think about it? How does the couple handle sensitive issues such as religion? And surely cultural differences can create misunderstandings that a same-race couple may not have to deal with?

16   "Our parents are fine with it, but at first we didn't know if the older generation would be," says Min.

17   David claims his family is more traditional than Min's relations. "We were going out some time before I told my grandmother. But that's because she's 90, so she's very old-fashioned. I think a lot of differences aren't really to do with the culture, I think it's the way the families are: like, telling my grandmother wouldn't be difficult because I'm Irish—it's because my family are a very conservative family."

18

Cristina's father found out she was leaving for Ireland only the night before her flight. "Letting me go to another country for a guy is just a no-no, it's against my Filipino culture. I'm sure Dad was heart-broken—there was crying."

19   It seems that religion is a major factor where parents are concerned. Hana's Muslim father doesn't approve of her dating. "My Dad doesn't know. We had a little incident last

summer where there was talk of it and my Dad said 'you can't be doing this'. My Mom knows about my boyfriend, she's English." She wonders how her father can expect her to get married if she doesn't date.

20   Hana says her father is more liberal than most Muslim fathers and doesn't approve of arranged marriages as such. "I don't know whether it's his Indian mentality or whether it's the Muslim way of going about things. He probably wants [me to marry] a Muslim-Indian boy."

21   Eric and his parents are worried that Hana's father doesn't know about their relationship. "It bothers the hell out of him, and his parents really want to meet my parents but they can't yet," says Hana.

22   Cultural and linguistic diversities may have attracted them to each other in the first place but those differences have been the cause of communication barriers.

23   It took Cristina some time to get used to the Irish accent and the Irish way of saying things. Nick gives an example. "We say 'c'mere for a sec' when we mean to say 'listen' and she would say 'but I am here!' Now she just says it to annoy me."

24   Hana thinks accents are a cause for fascination more than a problem in her relationship with her American boyfriend. "English is my mother tongue. My Mom comes from Yorkshire, they have really broad, thick accents—he's quite fascinated by that. English humour is very different to American humour; we say things more sarcastically, so sometimes he doesn't get what I'm laughing about."

25   For an English major, Joana still feels that language is the main barrier in their relationship. "When I get upset I have a lot of trouble expressing myself; I think Eoin doesn't understand me. I love Portuguese sayings and I can't express them in English. Also I'm not funny at all in English but I'm hilarious in Portuguese: I never made anyone laugh in English!"

26   Most couples trying to nurture intercultural relationships here find Ireland provides a congenial environment, and none of these young couples have had negative reactions from the public.

27   However, many feel Ireland has a long way to go before it can completely acknowledge and integrate interracial relationships. "We don't see any couples who are mixed. We do look out for them but we've never seen a Filipino with an Irish guy in Dublin," says Nick.

28   Cristina feels that sometimes Nick openly make offensive jokes about her ethnicity. "He sees me more as a Filipino than a Canadian. In just a flash he robs my Canadian citizenship off me," she says. "In Ireland race is equal to nationality but to us race and nationality are different things. I understand now that he's in a country that's not very multicultural yet; having lived in Canada makes me understand that."

29 She was taken by surprise recently when she saw a mixed-mannequin family in a display window at a large department store.

30 "There was a white female mannequin, a black male mannequin and a child mannequin of mixed race. So much effort was put into it, even down to their hair!" she exclaims.

31 Cristina says there seems to be a faster racial integration among the dolls than among the real people in Ireland. "She laughs every time she sees one; they've had them in Canada for years," adds Nick. "She even made me take a photograph of it."

(Words: 1387)

Exercise I Discussion

Directions: Please discuss the following questions in pairs or groups.

1. What do you think of China's societal tolerance of intercultural relationship?
2. What is it that attracts young people from different countries, cultures and religious persuasions to each other?
3. Do you think couples from mixed backgrounds suffer more marital problems?

Exercise II Writing

Directions: Write a composition about how harmony is achieved by harnessing conflicts between countries or nations in about 200 words.

UNIT SEVEN

ETHNICITY, GENDER AND GAY MARRIAGE

*T*arget of the Unit

☞ To get a glimpse of social problems where ethnicity, gender and gay marriage are concerned
☞ To practice reading skills
☞ To enlarge your vocabulary

1) LEAD IN

Directions: In this unit, you will read 3 passages about gender and ethnicity in the American society; you will find a lot of problems that the Americans experience in their daily life; as you read you reflect upon those points that strike you as most interesting to you.

2) DISCUSSION

Do you think men and women are equal in social life? Can you give some examples to support your idea?

Text A

I Won't Die for Equality

By Cristina Odone

*W*arming-up Exercises

☞ What does equality between men and women mean?
☞ Do you agree that Chinese women enjoy greater freedom than their foreign peers?

First reading

Directions: Now please read the following passage as fast as you can and summarize the main idea.

1   Seventy-five years ago all British women were finally given what all British men had been granted 10 years earlier—the right to vote. First off the blocks to mark the occasion has been, oddly, the *Sun* (that same organ, ironically, mostly "celebrates" women's emancipation with a naked interest in their **bulging** breasts and shapely bums).

2   That no one else has yet seemed to notice reflects the fact that the winning side in the equality war doesn't want to waste precious time crowing. They want to get on with dealing the most humiliating defeat upon the remaining enemy: foes such as those employers who pay women less than comparable men; the corporations with an all-male hierarchy at the top; and of course the men who tiresomely persist in sexist words or behavior.

> **bulge** *v.* to stick out in a rounded shape, especially because sth is very full or too tight 鼓起
> **Amazon** *n.* a strong and tall woman 强壮高大的女性
> **cluster bomb** *n. phr.* a bomb that sends out smaller bombs when it explodes 集束炸弹

3   Like the military. A report last week slammed the Army for sexism, complaining that women are called "girls"—quite different, the authors said, from referring to the troops as "our boys". "Boys", it seems, is a good, encouraging, matey kind of word. "Girls", by contrast, is derogatory and demeaning. This was only to be expected, the authors pointed out, from an institution that enjoys "partial" exemption from equal opportunities legislation—and thus can exclude its "girls" from some direct combat positions. How chauvinist can you get?

4   But hold on: do women really want to turn Dad's Army into Mum's Army, a posse of latter-day **Amazons** braving the front line, cheek by jowl with their male counterparts? We don't want to stand beside the boys and fire rifles into the whites of Iraqi eyes. Nor are we gasping for a chance to be blasted to smithereens by a **cluster bomb**. I may not be crazy about being called 'girl', but that doesn't mean I want to be mowed down with the 'boys' in the killing fields.

5   Yet this kind of job-equalising—if Jack can do it, Jill sure as hell can do it better—has long been cherished by social planners, feminist or not. For decades, men-only **enclaves** gave women their battle cry: let me in there! The exclusion zone in those days ranged from smart clubs, manual work, the Church of England and the armed forces.

6   Now it has shrunk to a few moth-eaten armchairs in clubland; the golfers' paradise—the Royal and Ancient Club of St Andrews; the Roman Catholic priesthood; and front-line combat. The head of the Stock Exchange is a woman, female plumbers are growing in numbers (including that Oxford graduate, Nicola Gillison, who made headlines recently because she ditched her consultancy job for a mole **wrench**), and one in 12 of the Army is female. As for women lorry drivers, that should be no surprise. Women drivers have such a sterling record that insurance companies now offer cheaper premiums in turn for the promise that no man will come anywhere near the four wheels of their car.

7   Given such progress, only rabid equalizers would argue that they cannot rest until women have the right to be windbagged by some old **geezer** reading *Horse and Hound* by the fire; or risk death or a war wound through their rightful place on the front line.

8   Social engineering that fixes men and women in the same post, at all costs, makes no sense. As the foreigner chewed his dumplings at some dire Intourist restaurant in the Soviet Union, his (or her) surprised gaze might alight upon the workers outside in their drab overalls. Who were those stocky muscular figures clambering up the scaffolding with buckets of primrose yellow paint to freshen up the crumbling facades of the surrounding buildings? Women. Who was heaving the garbage containers into the dilapidated rubbish truck? Women. Who was shoveling up the piles of dirt and grit left in the melted snow by the side of the road? Women.

9   And what of the Israeli army, which believes women **sabras** as well as men should face enemy fire? That idea has proved a disaster—with men behaving suicidally to protect the women, casualties mounting, and the government now considering legislation to keep women away from the front. It's been a dire tale in the American military too, with physical strength tests rigged to accommodate women soldiers who with the best will in the world cannot throw a hand grenade to a safe distance.

> **enclave** *n.* a small area that is within a larger area where people of a different kind or nationality live 飞地（被外国领地包围的土地）
> **wrench** *n.* a metal tool that you use for turning nuts 扳手
> **geezer** *n.* (*BrE*) a man 人
> **sabra** *n.* (*esp US*) Israeli Jew bon in Israel 土生土长的以色列人
> **GI** *n.* a soldier in the US army, especially during the Second World War 美国大兵

10   There is nothing wrong with a handful of super-tough modern day **GI** Janes being

hooked on Jane's Guide to Extra Lethal Infantry Weapons, or wasting their weekends playing war games; the modern military needs women to boost its flagging recruits, and if supply now matches demands, I am sure we can all rest more easily in the shadow of the Axis of Evil.

11 But a woman does not need to be in the firing line to feel as good as a man. That is an equality too far.

(Words: 807)

• **Second Reading** •

Directions: Read the text again more carefully to find enough information for Exercises I, II & III.

Exercise I True or False

Directions: Please state whether the following statements are true or false (T/F) according to what you've found in the text.

1. British women gained the right to vote ten years later than all British men.
2. It was the Sun that first published the news of women getting the right to vote, which was the most natural thing.
3. To get the right to vote is far from enough for women.
4. Women don't want to be killed with men on the battlefield to show they are equal.
5. Only feminists have been working for the equality of women and men in job hunting.
6. Now men-only enclaves have shrunk to only a few areas.
7. Women have been working as heads of the Stock Exchange, plumbers, soldiers except drivers.
8. In order to protect female soldiers, men suffered more casualties on battlefield.
9. American women soldiers do worse because they even cannot throw a hand grenade to a safe distance.
10. There are some women who are crazy about war and fighting.

Exercise II   Word Inference

Directions: Often you can guess the meaning of a word/expression by reading the words around it. Please read the given sentence to see how each word/expression in bold type is used in the text. Then choose the answer that is closest in meaning to the bold-faced word/expression.

1. That no one else has yet seemed to notice reflects the fact that the winning side in the equality war doesn't want to waste precious time **crowing**.
   A. brag
   B. celebrate
   C. discuss
   D. shout

2. They want to get on with dealing the most humiliating defeat upon the remaining enemy: foes such as those employers who pay women less than comparable men; the corporations with an all-male hierarchy at the top; and of course the men who **tiresomely** persist in sexist words or behavior.
   A. annoyingly
   B. happily
   C. anxiously
   D. busily

3. A report last week **slammed** the Army for sexism, complaining that women are called "girls"—quite different, the authors said, from referring to the troops as "our boys".
   A. talk about
   B. beat
   C. criticize
   D. sing praise of

4. "Boys", it seems, is a good, encouraging, **matey** kind of word. "Girls", by contrast, is derogatory and demeaning.
   A. encouraging
   B. friendly
   C. good
   D. masculine

5. "Boys", it seems, is a good, encouraging, matey kind of word. "Girls", by contrast, is derogatory and **demeaning**.
   A. degrading
   B. critical
   C. hard
   D. sharp

6. But hold on: do women really want to turn Dad's Army into Mum's Army, a **posse** of latter-day Amazons braving the front line, cheek by jowl with their male counterparts?
   A. beauty
   B. daughter
   C. female
   D. group

7. But hold on: do women really want to turn Dad's Army into Mum's Army, a posse of latter-day Amazons braving the front line, **cheek by jowl** with their male counterparts?
   A. fight
   B. very close
   C. intimate
   D. happy

8. Given such progress, only **rabid** equalizers would argue that they cannot rest until women have the right to be windbagged by some old geezer reading *Horse and Hound* by the fire; or risk death or a war wound through their rightful place on the front line.

   A. extreme   B. abnormal
   C. reluctant   D. fair

9. Who were those stocky muscular figures clambering up the scaffolding with buckets of primrose yellow paint to freshen up the **crumbling** facades of the surrounding buildings?

   A. dirty   B. poor
   C. decaying   D. dark

10. It's been a **dire** tale in the American military too, with physical strength tests rigged to accommodate women soldiers who with the best will in the world cannot throw a hand grenade to a safe distance.

    A. exciting   B. similar
    C. better   D. terrible

Exercise III Discussion

Directions: Please discuss the following questions in pairs or groups.

1. Do you agree with the author that to fight in the army is "an equality too far"? To what extent should men and women be equal?
2. Do you think you can do something to help women achieve total equality with men?

Text B

Blacks, Whites and Love
By Nicholas Kristof

Warming-up Exercises

☞ Can entertainment industry always reflect society?

☞ Should entertainment industry reflect society? Should it contain any moral, any significant message, or just for amusement?

• First reading •

Directions: Now please read the following passage as fast as you can and summarize the main idea.

1   One gauge of the progress we've made in American race relations in recent decades is the growing number of blacks and whites who have integrated their hearts and ended up marrying each other. As of the 2000 census, 6 percent of married black men had a white wife, and 3 percent of married black women had a white husband. Huge majorities of both blacks and whites say they approve of interracial marriages. One survey found that 40 percent of Americans had dated someone of a different race.

2   But it's hard to argue that America is becoming more colorblind when we're still missing one **benchmark**: ___A___.

3   For all the gains in race relations, romance on the big screen between a black man and a white woman remains largely a **taboo**. Americans themselves may be falling in love with each other without regard to color, but the movie industry is still too craven to imitate life. Or perhaps the studios are too busy pushing the limits on sex, nudity and violence to portray something really **kinky**, like colorblind love.

> **benchmark** *n.* sth that is used as a standard by which other things can be judged or measured 水准点
> **taboo** *n.* a social or religious custom prohibiting or restricting a particular practice or forbidding association with a particular person, place, or thing 禁忌
> **kinky** *adj.* having or showing unusual ways of getting sexual excitement 怪异的
> **chaste** *adj.* simple and plain in style 贞洁的，质朴的
> **archetype** *n.* an original model on which something is patterned 原型

4   Back in 1967, "Guess Who's Coming to Dinner" helped chip away at taboos by showing a black man and white woman scandalizing their parents with their **chaste** love. In 2005 we have a new version of "Guess Who", but it only underscores how little progress we've made.

5   The latest "Guess Who" is about a white man in love with a black woman, and that's a comfortable old **archetype** from days when slave owners inflicted themselves on slave women. Hollywood has portrayed romances between white men and (usually light-complexioned) black women, probably calculating that any good ol' boy seeing Billy Bob

109

Thornton embracing Halle Berry in "Monster's Ball" is filled not with disgust but with envy.

___B___. At least 41 states at one time had laws banning interracial marriage. A 1958 poll found that 96 percent of whites disapproved of marriages between blacks and whites.

That same year, in North Carolina, two black boys, a 7-year-old named Fuzzy Simpson and a 9-year-old named Hanover Thompson, were arrested after a white girl kissed Hanover. The two boys were convicted of attempted rape. As Randall Kennedy notes in his book "Interracial Intimacies," Fuzzy was sentenced to 12 years, and Hanover to 14 years. ___C___.

___D___. That was the year that the daughter of Dean Rusk, then secretary of state, married a black man. Secretary Rusk proudly walked his daughter down the aisle (after warning President Lyndon Johnson of the political risks), and *Time* magazine put the couple on its cover. That was also the year of "Guess Who's Coming to Dinner" and of a Supreme Court ruling striking down miscegenation laws.

Yet right from the beginning, the entertainment industry has lagged society in its racial mores. Films and television have always been squeamish about race: in 1957, on Alan Freed's ABC show, the black singer Frankie Lymon was seen dancing with a white woman. ABC promptly canceled the show. There have been just a few mainstream movies with black men romancing white women, lower-profile films like "One Night Stand". More typically, you get a film like "Hitch", where the studio pairs a black man with a Latina.

> aisle *n*. a long passage between rows of seats in a church, plane, theatre, etc., or between rows of shelves in a shop 走廊，过道

___E___, and one breakthrough might come late next year with the possible release of "Emma's War"—a movie that 20th Century Fox is considering, in which a white woman—Nicole Kidman is being discussed—marries an African. It's great that Hollywood is close to catching up to Shakespeare's "Othello".

Let's hope that Hollywood will finally dare to be as iconoclastic as its audiences. It's been half a century since *Brown v. Board of Education* led to the integration of American schools, but the breakdown of the barriers of love will be a far more consequential and transformative kind of integration—not least because it's spontaneous and hormonal rather than imposed and legal.

(Words: 722)

• Second Reading •

Directions: Read the text again more carefully to find enough information for Exercises I, II, III & IV.

Exercise I Understanding Text Organization

Directions: You may find there are a few sentences (segments) missing from the passage. Read the article through and decide where the following sentences should go.

1. Off screen, the change has been dizzying
2. When will Hollywood dare release a major movie in which Denzel Washington and Reese Witherspoon fall passionately in love?
3. Popular entertainment shapes our culture as well as reflects it
4. Pressure from President Dwight Eisenhower eventually secured the boys' release
5. Then the mood began to change, and 1967 was the turning point

Exercise II Multiple-Choice Questions

Directions: Please choose the best answer to the following questions.

1. Why doesn't the movie industry in US depict romance between a black man and a white woman?
    A. Because the movie industry does not dare to do so.
    B. Because the law of many states does not allow it to do so.
    C. Because the audience does not like to see such romance on the screen.
    D. Because the movie industry is not interested in it.
2. What is the purpose of the author by comparing "Guess Who's Coming to Dinner" with the 2005 version?
    A. To show that the movie industry is still engaged in presenting the interracial

marriages.

  B. To introduce the new movie.

  C. To show that we made little progress during the decades.

  D. To form a contrast between what the movie industry is doing with real life.

3. Why did ABC cancel the show?

  A. Because it lagged behind society.

  B. Because it did not like current racial mores.

  C. Because it didn't want to show a black singer dancing with a white woman.

  D. Because it was not the mainstream of television.

4. What's the significance of "Emma's War"?

  A. It shows one breakthrough that Hollywood is going to make in depicting interracial love.

  B. It should be a big hit since Nicole Kidman is going to be the leading lady in the movie.

  C. It is going to catch up with the greatest drama of Shakespeare.

  D. It shapes our culture as well as reflects it.

5. What can we infer from the passage?

  A. The author is quite optimistic about the future of integration.

  B. The author is quite pessimistic about the future of integration.

  C. It is hoped that the breakdown of the barriers of love should be ensured by law.

  D. Hollywood is more conservative in interracial love than its audience.

Exercise III Word Inference

Directions: Often you can guess the meaning of a word/expression by reading the words around it. Please read the given sentence to see how each word/expression in bold type is used in the text. Then choose the answer that is closest in meaning to the bold-faced word/expression.

1. One **gauge** of the progress we've made in American race relations in recent decades is the growing number of blacks and whites who have integrated their hearts and ended up marrying each other.

   A. part   B. example

   C. cause   D. measurement

2. Americans themselves may be falling in love with each other without regard to color, but the movie industry is still too **craven** to imitate life.
   A. cowardly   B. lazy
   C. busy   D. brave

3. Back in 1967, "Guess Who's Coming to Dinner" helped **chip away at** taboos by showing a black man and white woman scandalizing their parents with their chaste love. In 2005 we have a new version of "Guess Who", but it only underscores how little progress we've made.
   A. develop   B. get rid of
   C. establish   D. defend

4. Back in 1967, "Guess Who's Coming to Dinner" helped chip away at taboos by showing a black man and white woman **scandalizing** their parents with their chaste love. In 2005 we have a new version of "Guess Who", but it only underscores how little progress we've made.
   A. please   B. sadden
   C. shock   D. challenge

5. Back in 1967, "Guess Who's Coming to Dinner" helped chip away at taboos by showing a black man and white woman scandalizing their parents with their chaste love. In 2005 we have a new version of "Guess Who", but it only **underscores** how little progress we've made.
   A. emphasize   B. show
   C. exhibit   D. prove

6. The latest "Guess Who" is about a white man in love with a black woman, and that's a comfortable old archetype from days when slave owners **inflicted themselves on** slave women.
   A. enjoy   B. dare
   C. beat   D. harass

7. That was also the year of "Guess Who's Coming to Dinner" and of a Supreme Court ruling striking down **miscegenation** laws.
   A. marriage   B. illegal marriage
   C. legal marriage   D. interracial marriage

8. Yet right from the beginning, the entertainment industry has lagged society in its racial **mores**.
   A. moral values   B. standards
   C. ideas   D. views

113

9. Films and television have always been **squeamish** about race: in 1957, on Alan Freed's ABC show, the black singer Frankie Lymon was seen dancing with a white woman.

 A. careful   B. daring

 C. sensitive   D. careless

10. Let's hope that Hollywood will finally dare to be as **iconoclastic** as its audiences.

 A. numb   B. idealistic

 C. optimistic   D. sharp

Exercise IV Discussion

Directions: Please discuss the following questions in pairs or groups.

1. Do you agree with the author's conclusion? What do you expect Hollywood to do in the near future about interracial marriage?
2. What is the purpose of the author by comparing "Emma's War" with Shakespeare's "Othello"?

Text C

Oregon Supreme Court Invalidates Same-Sex Marriages

By Sarah Kershaw

1 Oregon's highest court ruled yesterday that 3,000 same-sex marriages performed a year ago in one county were unlawful, saying that the county had overstepped its authority and that the licenses it had issued were unconstitutional under Oregon law.

2 The justices on the Oregon Supreme Court focused heavily in their highly anticipated opinion on a vote by Oregonians in November that widely approved a constitutional amendment to define marriage as a union between one man and one woman. They also ruled that even before the approval Oregon law had already rendered the same-sex marriages, conducted last March and April in Multnomah County, illegal.

3 "County officials were entitled to have their doubts about the constitutionality of limiting

marriage to opposite-sex couples," Justice W. Michael Gillette wrote for the court. "But marriage and the laws governing it are matters of statewide, not local, concern."

4   The ruling said, "Today, marriage in Oregon—an institution once limited to opposite-sex couples only by statute—now is so limited by the State Constitution, as well."

5   Supporters of same-sex marriage said that they would not abandon their quest for full marriage rights, but that in the meantime they would work to win passage of bills that would allow civil unions for gay couples.

6   Vermont is the sole state that sanctions civil unions, although legislatures in Oregon and Connecticut are debating them. Massachusetts is the lone state where same-sex marriage is legal.

7   "We are going to continue to advocate for civil unions," said Rebekah Kassell, a spokeswoman for Basic Rights Oregon, a plaintiff in the Oregon case, "and we are confident that the courts will end the exclusion of same-sex couples from these protections for their relationships and their families."

8   Ms. Kassell said thousands of gay Oregonians, including the daughter of Mayor Tom Potter of Portland, had celebrated their first wedding anniversaries.

9   "I feel our marriage is solid regardless of the decision today," the daughter, Katie Potter, 40, said in a telephone interview. "I realize and acknowledge that the state is not going to accept it and acknowledge it. But we were married, and I'll never again feel like what it - surprisingly - felt like after getting married that day."

10   Ms. Potter and her partner of 15 years, Pam Moen, 53, who have two daughters, 5 and 2, were married on March 3, 2004, as soon as word spread that Multnomah County, which includes Portland, was issuing the marriage licenses to gay couples.

11   "It was enjoying that moment of having, suddenly, someone say there is validity to this, outside of us," Ms. Potter said.

12   Opponents of same-sex marriage said they were particularly irked by Multnomah's issuing licenses not sanctioned by the state.

13   "The vast middle of the electorate out there was always worried that there might be some secret gay agenda," said Kelly Clark, a lawyer who represented Oregon's Defense of Marriage Coalition in the case. "And, lo and behold, there was a secret gay agenda."

14   "I think they set their cause back," Mr. Clark added.

15   Lawyers for the state argued before the court that while the decision to issue the licenses was unconstitutional, gay Oregonians should have the same benefits as married couples.

16   Gov. Theodore R. Kulongoski, along with several state senators, introduced a bill this week that would allow civil unions under state law.

17   "The state's position from the outset was that the fundamental issue was whether or not same-sex couples were entitled to the rights and privileges of marriage, not just the institution of marriage itself," said Kevin Neely, a spokesman for the Oregon attorney general, Hardy Myers.

18   Oregon is one of 17 states with constitutional amendments that define marriage as between a man and a woman, according to the Human Rights Campaign. At least 18 state legislatures are considering similar measures, according to the National Conference of State Legislatures.

19   Some states have also taken up the question of what benefits to extend to domestic partners, including gay couples. Experts say California has come closest to offering virtually all the benefits of civil unions.

20   Legal cases on whether gay men and lesbians can marry are winding their way through state and county courts in at least six states, according to the Human Rights Campaign. They include New York, Washington and California, where thousands of same-sex marriages were performed in San Francisco though later voided the California Supreme Court.

21   National gay rights groups insist that same-sex marriage remains their ultimate goal, even if the focus has recently turned to civil unions in some states.

22   "We recognize that like any social change in this country, it's going to be a long-term fight," Joe Solmonese, president of the Human Rights Campaign, said. "One that will be marked by taking three steps forward and two steps back."

(Words: 1242)

Exercise I Discussion

Directions: Please discuss the following questions in pairs or groups.

1. Which side do you take—to allow civil unions for gay couples or to ban same-sex marriage?
2. Why does the president of the Human Rights Campaign believe that the fight is going to be a long-term one?
3. Do you think gay couples should be offered benefits?

Exercise II Writing

Directions: The articles in this unit are related to ethnicity, gender and gay marriage. Write a composition on any one of the above key terms in about 200 words.

UNIT EIGHT

STRIVING FOR GOALS

Target of the Unit

☞ To get a glimpse of the American character that drives them to move towards their goals
☞ To practice reading skills
☞ To enlarge your vocabulary

1) LEAD IN

Directions: In this unit, you will read 3 passages about how Americans, whether they are at the top of the society or at the grassroots, are striving to win their rights—the right to rule or the right to work.

2) DISCUSSION

Do you have any idea about the American society in so far as their right to employment is concerned?

Text A

Let's Try Baloney

By Eleanor Clift

Warming-up Exercises

☞ What apparent differences have you noticed in terms of Bush and Clinton administration?
☞ How do your parents solve a family crisis?

First reading

Directions: Now please read the following passage as fast as you can and summarize the main idea.

1   Things aren't getting better in Bush land. They had a horrific week with the election results. Virginia, a Red State, elected a new governor, Tim Kaine, a Democrat to the left of current Gov. Mark Warner, who's now a hot presidential prospect as a Democrat who can bridge the divide between Red and Blue America.

2   Events were no better elsewhere. Bombings of hotels in Amman, Jordan, begged the question: Why can't we capture Abu Musab al-Zarqawi, the Jordanian-born insurgent leader in Iraq suspected of carrying out the attacks—or Osama bin Laden for that matter? Al-Zarqawi moves beyond the borders of Iraq to become a regional threat while Vice President Dick Cheney, a veteran of multiple draft deferments, battles Sen. John McCain, a former POW, for pushing an amendment to the defense **appropriations** bill that puts the U.S. government on record opposing torture.

3   Something is deeply **askew** in the White House when the priorities are so off kilter. Unless events conspire to save President George W. Bush—Iraq turns around, the economy improves for average workers (not just oil execs), and the price of energy comes down—he is heading for a full meltdown, a scary prospect when you realize he's president for three more years. What's needed now is the political imagination to change direction, the way President Bill Clinton did after losing both the House and Senate in 1994.

> **appropriation** n. sth appropriated, especially public funds set aside for a specific purpose. 拨款
> **askew** adj. out of line, off center 斜的
> **atrophy** n. wasting way of the body or part of it through lack of nourishment or use（身体或身体某部分因缺乏营养或不常使用而）萎缩

4   Bush went on the offensive Friday, saying in a Veteran's Day speech that critics of his Iraq policies are undercutting American soldiers on the front lines. He also attacked Democrats who claim that pre-war intelligence was manipulated by the White House. But evidence to the contrary will make this a hard sell.

5   The people who most want Bush to succeed are the alumni of his father's administration, and they are in despair over the state of the White House. One former diplomat after three glasses of wine at an embassy dinner confessed that he has a recurring image of the White House as a crab with seven **atrophied** legs and one over-developed leg, which would be Karl Rove, pulling everything along. "If he goes, there's nothing left." Exhausted and demoralized Bush aides are turning on each other and leaking stories to the press, a breakdown in discipline

that was common in the Clinton White House, but new to the Bush operation. Friends of the senior Bush are blaming Cheney for usurping too much power, but that's why they wanted him there, as a **minder** for the man-child who should never have been made president.

6   This is a battle between the Bushes of Kennebunkport and the Bushes of Crawford, and who prevails will determine which direction Bush 43 goes for the rest of his term. The Connecticut crowd is headed by Bush 41 with Brent Scowcroft, the former national security adviser, speaking for the father, James Baker the **consigliore**, and chief-of-staff Andy Card their mole. Scowcroft has terminally offended the White House with his anti-Iraq war views. "He might as well be dead," says the former diplomat. "If you say anything publicly, you're frozen out. You have to show comity toward them, or they won't listen to you."

> **minder** n. someone who is employed to protect another person 看管者
> **consigliore** n. The correct spelling is "consigliere", an Italian term for "adviser" or "counselor" 这是个意大利词, 当拼写为 "consigliere", 意思是 "counselor", 即 "顾问" 之意
> **pollster** n. someone who works for a company that prepares and asks questions to find out what people think about a particular subject 民意调查者

7   Suiting up on the Crawford side is Rove, and of course Bush 43, who reinforce each other. If Bush sticks with Rove and goes to the right, there's a ceiling on his popularity at best of 45 percent. If he moves to the center, like the Bush 41 crowd would like, the base collapses and he doesn't necessarily pick up votes in the center. The administration is too far gone, the problems intractable.

8   When Clinton got into trouble, he reached outside his White House and secretly consulted with **pollster** Dick Morris, whose strategy of "triangulation" positioned Clinton

between the Democrats and the Republican Congress, and revived his presidency. The elder Bush's allies are pushing to bring in two or three people who can talk to Bush and help fashion fresh approaches to the nation's problems in the State of the Union address early next year. Who might those people be? After a long silence, the diplomat suggested Jim Baker, who has come to the rescue before, but who is better suited to working behind the scenes. The Right distrusts him and would rebel if they saw Baker's fingerprints.

9 The other name offered was Condoleeza Rice, who Bush calls "mother hen." She spends time with him—biking, **pumping iron** and taking walks—or at least she did when she was national security adviser and didn't travel so much. "He needs people who affirm him," said the diplomat, recalling Harriet Miers's note to then Gov. Bush that he was "deserving of the greatest respect." In this diplomat's assessment, having known the Bush family, respect is the key word. Bush for years was the ne'er do well son of a respected, duty-bound father, and he's still playing catch-up in the family **Oedipal** drama.

> **pump iron** v. phr. (infml) weight lifting 举重
> **Oedipal** adj. related to an Oedipus complex 恋母情结的，（希腊神话）俄狄浦斯的
> **baloney** n. (Slang) foolishness; nonsense 愚蠢

10 Talking to Bush requires what diplomats call the "baloney sandwich approach." It works like this: Your spouse has run up the credit cards. Confronting her will provoke a fight. So you flatter her, tell her what a great wife and mother she is; then present this teeny little problem the two of you can work together to solve because you love her so much. Bush's world has collapsed in on him. It's time to try something new, even if it's **baloney**.

(Words: 937)

· Second Reading ·

Directions: Read the text again more carefully to find enough information for Exercises I, II, III & IV.

Exercise I True or False

Directions: Please state whether the following statements are true or false (T/F) according to what you've found in the text.

1. Tim Kaine is now a hot presidential prospect as a Democrat who can bridge the divide between Red and Blue America.
2. Osama bin Laden moves beyond the borders of Iraq to become a regional threat while Vice President Dick Cheney battles Sen. John McCain.
3. What's needed now is the political imagination to change direction, the way President Bill Clinton did after losing both the House and Senate in 1994.
4. Bush's Veteran's Day speech is accepted by the American citizens very well.

5. The alumni of Bush's father's administration are in despair over the state of the White House.

6. One former diplomat at an embassy luncheon confessed that he has a recurring image of the White House is like a crab with seven atrophied legs and one over-developed leg.

7. Friends of the senior Bush are blaming Cheney for usurping too much power.

8. This is a battle between the Bushes of Kennebunkport and the Bushes of Crawford.

9. When Bush got into trouble, he reached outside his White House and secretly consulted with pollster Dick Morris.

10. The elder Bush's allies showed little interest in trying to bring in people who can help Bush fashion fresh approaches to the nation's problems.

Exercise II Word Inference

Directions: Often you can guess the meaning of a word/expression by reading the words around it. Please read the given sentence to see how each word/expression in bold type is used in the text. Then choose the answer that is closest in meaning to the bold-faced word/expression.

1. Virginia, a Red State, elected a new governor, Tim Kaine, a Democrat to the left of **current** Gov. Mark Warner, who's now a hot presidential prospect as a Democrat who can bridge the divide between Red and Blue America.

    A. temporary   B. present
    C. contemporary   D. ephemeral

2. They had a **horrific** week with the election results.

    A. exciting   B. horrible
    C. sad   D. sweet

3. Something is deeply askew in the White House when the priorities are so **off kilter**.

    A. obvious   B. abnormal
    C. high   D. advantageous

4. Unless events **conspire** to save President George W. Bush—Iraq turns around, the economy improves for average workers (not just oil execs), and the price of energy comes down—he is heading for a full meltdown, a scary prospect when you realize he's president for three more years.

    A. (of events) act together   B. make secret plans
    C. plan to do something bad   D. plan to do something illegally

122

5. Unless events conspire to save President George W. Bush—Iraq turns around, the economy improves for average workers (not just oil execs), and the price of energy comes down—he is heading for a full **meltdown**, a scary prospect when you realize he's president for three more years.

   A. disaster
   B. rush
   C. failure
   D. surplus

6. Friends of the senior Bush are blaming Cheney for **usurping** too much power, but that's why they wanted him there, as a minder for the man-child who should never have been made president.

   A. use
   B. seize
   C. abuse
   D. have

7. This is a battle between the Bushes of Kennebunkport and the Bushes of Crawford, and who **prevails** will determine which direction Bush 43 goes for the rest of his term. The Connecticut crowd is headed by Bush 41 with Brent Scowcroft, the former national security adviser, speaking for the father, James Baker the consigliore, and chief-of-staff Andy Card their mole.

   A. popularize
   B. triumph
   C. bewilder
   D. confuse

8. If you say anything publicly, you're frozen out. You have to show **comity** toward them, or they won't listen to you.

   A. committal
   B. cordiality
   C. cowardice
   D. comic

9. The administration is too far gone, the problems **intractable**.

   A. docile
   B. knotty
   C. intact
   D. intangible

10. The elder Bush's allies are pushing to bring in two or three people who can talk to Bush and help **fashion** fresh approaches to the nation's problems in the State of the Union address early next year.

    A. design
    B. popularize
    C. influence
    D. reform

Exercise III Discussion

Directions: Please discuss the following questions in pairs or groups.

1. What is "baloney sandwich approach"? Why does the author say "talking to Bush requires what diplomats call the 'baloney sandwich approach'"?
2. Did the author take a position in this article? How do you know?

Text B

Thousands Rally for Immigrants' Rights

By Tim Molloy

From The Associated Press, March 24, 2006

Warming-up Exercises

☞ How much do you know about immigration?
☞ Which country is an ideal country for people to migrate to?

• First reading •

Directions: Now please read the following passage as fast as you can and summarize the main idea.

1   LOS ANGELES (AP) — Thousands of people across the country protested Friday against legislation cracking down on illegal immigrants, with demonstrators in cities such as Los Angeles, Phoenix and Atlanta staging school walkouts, marches and work stoppages.

2   Congress is considering bills that would make it a felony to be in the United States illegally, impose new penalties on employers who hire illegal immigrants and erect fences along one-third of the U.S.-Mexican border. The proposals have angered many **Hispanics**.

3   ___A___, but the protests were largely peaceful, authorities said.

4   Chantal Mason, a sophomore at George Washington Preparatory High, said black students started a scuffle with Hispanic students as they left classes to take part in a protest.

5   "It was horrible, horrible," Mason said. "It's ridiculous that a bunch of black students would

> **Hispanics** *n.* a Spanish-speaking person; a US citizen or resident of Latin-American or Spanish descent 讲西班牙语的人，拉美裔或西班牙裔美国公民

jump on Latinos like that, knowing they're trying to get their freedom."

6 _____B_____, said Los Angeles district spokeswoman Monica Carazo.

7 In Phoenix, police said 20,000 demonstrators marched to the office of Republican Sen. Jon Kyl, co-sponsor of a bill that would give illegal immigrants up to five years to leave the country. The **turnout** clogged major **thoroughfares** in what officials said was one of the largest protests in the city's history. People also protested outside Kyl's Tucson office.

8 Kyl pointed out that most were speaking out against the House bill making it a felony to be an illegal immigrant, not his bill, which would also step up border enforcement and create a temporary guest-worker program.

9 "They (protesters) should be pleased that the Senate is probably going to address this in a much more comprehensive way," Kyl told the Tucson Citizen newspaper during a meeting with its editorial board.

10 In Los Angeles, more than 2,700 students from at least eight high schools and junior high schools walked out, district officials said. _____C_____.

11 Some of the students visited other high schools, trying to encourage additional students to join their protest, but some schools were locked down to keep students from leaving, Carazo said.

12 In Georgia, _____D_____.

13 That bill, which has yet to gain Senate approval, would deny state services to adults living in the U.S. illegally and impose a 5 percent **surcharge** on wire transfers from illegal immigrants.

14 _____E_____. Opponents say it unfairly targets workers meeting the demands of some of the state's largest industries.

15 Teodoro Maus, an organizer of the Georgia protest, estimated as many as 80,000 Hispanics did not show up for work. About 200 converged on the steps of the Georgia Capitol, some

> **turnout** n. (singular) the number of people who go to a party, meeting, or other organized event 聚集的人群
> **thoroughfare** n. the main road through a place such as a city or village 主要大街, 通衢
> **surcharge** n. an additional sum added to the usual amount or cost 附加费

125

wrapped in Mexican flags and holding signs reading: "Don't panic, we're Hispanic" and "We have a dream, too."

> panic v. to affect or be affected with panic 吓慌

16   Jennifer Garcia worried what would the proposal would do to her family. She said her husband is an illegal Mexican immigrant.

17   "If they send him back to Mexico, who's going to take care of them and me?" Garcia said of herself and her four children. "This is the United States. We need to come together and be a whole."

18   In Cleveland, about 100 protesters stood on the City Hall steps, waving Mexican flags and holding signs written in English and Spanish, and calling on Congress to create laws that respect immigrants as workers.

19   "This bill is anti-American," said David Quintan, 57, of Chile, who has lived in the United States for 30 years. "It's discriminatory not only to Latinos but to all immigrants. They're coming to work, not to steal or do terrorism. We are just workers."

(Words: 679)

· Second Reading ·

Directions: Read the text again more carefully to find enough information for Exercises I, II, III & IV.

Exercise I Understanding Text Organization

Directions: *You may find there are a few sentences (segments) missing from the passage. Read the article through and decide where the following sentences should go.*

1. The Los Angeles demonstration led to fights between black and Hispanic students at one high school

2. One black and one Hispanic student interceded to calm their classmates and help restore order
3. Some carried Mexican flags as they walked down the streets, police cruisers behind them
4. Activists said tens of thousands of workers did not show up at their jobs Friday after calls for a work stoppage to protest a bill passed by the Georgia House on Thursday
5. Supporters say the Georgia measure is vital to homeland security and frees up limited state services for people legally entitled to them

Exercise II Multiple-Choice Questions

Directions: Complete each of the following statements with the best choice given.

1. The protest of thousands of people across the country Friday _____.
    A. was against legislation cracking down on illegal immigrants
    B. led to fights between white and Hispanic students at one high school
    C. resulted in very violent fights at George Washington Preparatory High
    D. occurred in cities such as Los Angeles, Washington, D.C. and Atlanta
2. Demonstrators staged _____.
    A. school walkouts					B. marches
    C. work stoppages					D. all of above
3. _____was Los Angeles district spokeswoman.
    A. Jennifer Garcia					B. Chantal Mason
    C. Monica Carazo					D. David Quintan
4. Teodoro Maus, an organizer of the Georgia protest, estimated as many as _____ Hispanics did not show up for work in Georgia.
    A. 8,000							B. 80,000
    C. 18,000							D. 81,000
5. In _____, police said 20,000 demonstrators marched to the office of Republican Sen. Jon Kyl.
    A. Los Angeles						B. Georgia
    C. Cleveland						D. Phoenix

Exercise III Word Inference

Directions: Often you can guess the meaning of a word/expression by reading the words around it. Please read the given sentence to see how each word/expression in bold type is used in the text. Then choose the answer that is closest in meaning to the bold-faced word/expression.

1. Thousands of people across the country protested Friday against legislation cracking down on illegal immigrants, with demonstrators in cities such as Los Angeles, Phoenix and Atlanta **staging** school walkouts, marches and work stoppages.

    A. carry sth out
    B. carry sth on
    C. carry sth over
    D. carry sth through

2. Thousands of people across the country protested Friday against legislation cracking down on illegal immigrants, with demonstrators in cities such as Los Angeles, Phoenix and Atlanta staging school **walkouts**, marches and work stoppages.

    A. leaving job suddenly because you no longer want to do it
    B. stopping work as a protest
    C. leaving a place suddenly, esp. because you disapprove of sth
    D. leaving your school suddenly to go and live somewhere else

3. Congress is considering bills that would make it a **felony** to be in the United States illegally, impose new penalties on employers who hire illegal immigrants and erect fences along one-third of the U.S.-Mexican border.

    A. a misdemeanor
    B. a serious crime
    C. a serious misbehavior
    D. a small misconduct

4. Chantal Mason, a sophomore at George Washington Preparatory High, said black students started a **scuffle** with Hispanic students as they left classes to take part in a protest.

    A. wrestle
    B. conversation
    C. walkout
    D. fire

5. "It was horrible, horrible," Mason said. "It's ridiculous that a bunch of black students would **jump on** Latinos like that, knowing they're trying to get their freedom."

    A. scold
    B. attack
    C. criticize
    D. quarrel

128

6. One black and one Hispanic student **interceded** to calm their classmates and help restore order, said Los Angeles district spokeswoman Monica Carazo.

   A. intercept
   B. plead
   C. mediate
   D. intermingle

7. The turnout **clogged** major thoroughfares in what officials said was one of the largest protests in the city's history. People also protested outside Kyl's Tucson office.

   A. block
   B. occupy
   C. clean
   D. dirty

8. "They (protesters) should be pleased that the Senate is probably going to **address** this in a much more comprehensive way," Kyl told the Tucson Citizen newspaper during a meeting with its editorial board

   A. write directly to sb
   B. start trying to solve a problem
   C. make a formal speech to an audience
   D. write the address of sb

9. About 200 **converged** on the steps of the Georgia Capitol, some wrapped in Mexican flags and holding signs reading: "Don't panic, we're Hispanic" and "We have a dream, too."

   A. diverge
   B. divide
   C. meet
   D. branch

10. "It's **discriminatory** not only to Latinos but to all immigrants. They're coming to work, not to steal or do terrorism. We are just workers."

    A. discreet
    B. discursive
    C. discriminating
    D. discerning

Exercise IV Discussion

Directions: Please discuss the following questions in pairs or groups.

1. Why is immigration policy so important to the government?
2. Will the temporary guest-worker program be feasible in the U.S.? Why?

Text C

Tale of Two Presidents

By Richard Wolffe and Holly Bailey

1   The State of the Union was a tale of two presidents. One was gracious about his opponents, seeking common ground for the sake of the nation's future. The other accused his critics of being isolationists, pacifists, protectionists and unpatriotic.

2   One wanted the downfall of tyrants and dictators; the other wanted the downfall or transformation of elected governments in Iran and the Palestinian territories.

3   One wanted to extend tax cuts; the other wanted to cut deficits.

4   One was determined to promote America as the world leader in science; the other was determined to put strict limits on human-embryo research—restrictions that other countries have rejected.

5   Both presidents are of course one and the same: the often inspirational, often self-contradicting, George W. Bush. Democrats frequently mistake this split personality as some kind of giant game of bait-and-switch. But it's more accurate to think of it as the gap between Bush's idealistic self-image as a leader, and his realistic desire to do whatever it takes to win.

6   Part of President Bush genuinely wants to be fiscally responsible. Another part of him sorely wants to skewer Democrats on taxes in 2008 if they try to let his tax cuts expire. Part of President Bush genuinely wants to lead a harmonious and united nation in the long battle against Islamist terrorists. Another part of him sorely wants to silence his Democratic critics and portray them as weaklings in November.

7   Judging by their dozy response, the Democrats are ready to play their part. Many House Democrats on Tuesday could barely focus while their rival-in-chief was delivering his script for unseating them in the fall. Near the back of the chamber, Rep. Anthony Weiner, a Dem from New York, worked on a crossword puzzle as Bush made his way to the podium. Once Bush was on stage, Weiner and several of his colleagues broke out their BlackBerrys and spent most of the speech scrolling through e-mails and muttering to each other under their breaths, prompting Democratic leader Nancy Pelosi to hush them at one point.

8   Then again, the president's own party was hardly electrifying on Tuesday. When Bush made his rallying cry for fiscal discipline, his GOP troops offered only polite applause. Even the House leadership contenders John Boehner and John Shadegg, who have campaigned on the issue, failed to rise from their seats. There was similarly polite applause to Bush's call for a guest-worker program.

9   In stark contrast, the first person to jump out of his seat at the very mention of ethical standards was one Bob Ney. The Ohio congressman stepped down from his chairmanship of the House Administration Committee just two weeks ago because of his relationship with the indicted lobbyist Jack Abramoff.

10   Whether his party is in top form or not, Bush is returning to familiar ground in this election year. It's not just the substance of energy independence or health savings accounts. It's the style of his politics. In two election cycles, President Bush's combination of soaring rhetoric and street-fighting politics has resulted in victory at the polls. Now President Bush will use the same strategy to fight the 2006 elections—by calling for bipartisan support for the war on terror, while kneecapping Democrats as defeatist simpletons.

11   It seems to be working already. Many Democrats listening to Bush's address on Tuesday felt compelled to applaud his patriotism at several points, even when he was hammering them on Iraq. "To confront the great issues before us, we must act in a spirit of goodwill and respect for one another," Bush said early on, "and I will do my part." He did his part a little later by burying Jack Murtha, the hawkish House Democrat who called for the withdrawal of troops from Iraq. "There is a difference between responsible criticism that aims for success, and defeatism that refuses to acknowledge anything but failure," Bush declared, without naming anyone in the audience directly.

12   How Democrats respond is the critical test of whether they are ready to win an election. Judging by their official response, delivered by Virginia Gov. Tim Kaine, they would prefer to avoid almost all talk of foreign affairs. However, that choice may not be theirs, since the president has the bully pulpit and the country clearly remains at war.

13   Instead, their best hope lies in exploiting the contradictions of Bush's approach. The president's strategy of defeating terrorism with democracy faces fundamental challenges in the Palestinian territories, Lebanon and Iran. In all three places, terrorists and militants have attracted more popular support, not less, through the ballot box.

14   Democrats have a rare opening to be more hawkish than Bush on terrorism. They could argue, like Jordan, that the current goal must be to fight militants and terrorists—not to move towards more democracy. They could argue, like Bush himself in 2000, that the job of the U.S. military is to win war, not build nations.

15   Bush's current analysis of terrorism suggests he is unclear about what drives his mortal enemies or how best to kill them. Early on, the president suggested that terrorism was the result of a lack of democracy. "Dictatorships shelter terrorists, and feed resentment and radicalism, and seek weapons of mass destruction," he explained. Those dictatorships would obviously not include Pakistan or Saudi Arabia, whose governments are happy to shoot up Al Qaeda suspects.

16   Just seven sentences later, it turns out that terrorists aren't fighting dictators—they are fighting democracies. "No one can deny the success of freedom, but some men rage and fight against it," he said. Unlike the men of Hamas, of course, who seem to be enjoying freedom.

17   The president lumped together terrorists in Beslan, London and Iraq, as if they were the same. Yet the only common factor, apart from their bloodlust, is the religion of those involved. Chechen terrorists are hardly fighting against democratic government in their republic. The London bombers, in contrast, were British citizens, not Saudis hankering after the vote.

18   This is more than just muddled thinking. It's a sign that five years in office have left the White House straining under the weight of its own contradictions. Iraq was never meant to be a war about terrorists or democracy. It was a war launched to disarm a dictator with weapons of mass destruction. By lumping the two together out of political necessity, the White House seems to have lost focus on the single goal that voters really care about: killing off Al Qaeda. At least one side of President Bush understood that in 2001. The other side is trying to make sense of what happened since.

(Words: 1138)

Exercise I Discussion

Directions: Please discuss the following questions in pairs or groups.

1. How do you understand the title "a tale of two presidents"?
2. Do the authors take a position in writing their president? Give evidence from the text to explain.

Exercise II Writing

Directions: Write a composition about a success story of an American or a group of Americans in about 200 words.

GLOSSARY

A

acquisition	n.	someone or something acquired or added 增添的人或物
aficionado	n.	an enthusiastic admirer or follower; a fan ……迷
aisle	n.	a long passage between rows of seats in a church, plane, theatre, etc., or between rows of shelves in a shop 走廊，过道
Amazon	n.	a strong and tall woman 强壮高大的女性
appropriation	n.	sth appropriated, especially public funds set aside for a specific purpose 拨款
archetype	n.	an original model on which something is patterned 原型
archived	adj.	To place or store in an archive 存档的
askew	adj.	out of line, off center 斜的
assail	v.	to attack with or as if with violent blows; assault
atrophy	n.	wasting way of the body or part of it through lack of nourishment or use（身体或身体某部分因缺乏营养或不常使用而）萎缩
aversion	n.	dislike, repugnance 憎恶

B

baloney	n.	(Slang) foolishness; nonsense 愚蠢
bane	n.	sth that causes trouble or makes people unhappy 祸根
barge	n.	a large low boat with a flat bottom 大型平底船，驳船
BCLFC	abbr.	Birmingham City Ladies Football Club 伯明翰市女足俱乐部
beachhead	n.	an area of shore that has been taken from an enemy by force, and from which the army can prepare to attack a country（部队登陆后准备进攻时所建的）滩头阵地
behemoth	n.	sth enormous in size or power 庞大的
behold	v.	to see or look at sth 看呀
beleaguered	adj.	experiencing a lot of criticism and difficulties 处于困境的
benchmark	n.	sth that is used as a standard by which other things can be judged or measured 水准点

binge	n.	an unrestrained and often excessive indulgence; spree …… 热
book	v	(*sports*) to record the flagrant fouls of (a player) for possible disciplinary action, as in soccer 因犯规被记名
brandish	v.	to wave or flourish (a weapon, for example) menacingly
buff	n.	sb who is interested in wine, films, etc. and knows a lot about them 行家，爱好者
bulge	v.	to stick out in a rounded shape, especially because sth is very full or too tight 鼓起
buzzword	n.	a word or phrase from one special area of knowledge that people suddenly think is very important 热点词

C

Calypso	n.	a type of Caribbean song based on subjects of interest in the news 卡利普所，一种加勒比音乐形式，以当前新闻中关注话题为主题的歌曲
canny	adj.	clever, artful, crafty 狡黠的，很精的
charter	v	to pay a company for the use of their aircraft, boat, etc. 包租（飞机、轮船等）
chaste	adj.	simple and plain in style 贞洁的，质朴的
cheek by jowl	phr.	side by side; close together 亲近，亲密
cherry-pick	v.	to choose the best things or people you want from a group before anyone else has the chance to take them 抢先挑选
choreography	n.	the work of dance or ballet created and arranged by the choreographer 编导的作品
chug	v.	If a car, train, etc. chugs somewhere, it moves there slowly, with the engine making a repeated low sound 发着咔嚓声行驶
churning	adj.	moving about violently 动荡的
clientele	n.	all the clients of a shop/store, organization, etc. 客户
clog	v.	block, jam 拥堵
clout	n.	power or the authority to influence other people's decisions 力量
cluster bomb	n. phr.	a bomb that sends out smaller bombs when it explodes 集束炸弹
collaborate	v.	to work together with a person or group in order to achieve something, especially in science or art 合作
collage	n.	an artistic composition of materials and objects pasted over a surface, often with unifying lines and color 拼贴
collateral	n.	property or other goods that you promise to give someone if you cannot pay back the money they lend you 抵押
comity	n.	courteous behavior; politeness; civility

consigliore	n.	The correct spelling is "consigliere", an Italian ferm for "adviser" or "counselor" 这是个意大利词，当拼写为 "consigliere"，意思是 "counselor"，即 "顾问" 之意
converge	v.	to come together from different directions; meet 会合
counterpoint	n.	The technique of combining two or more melodic lines in such a way that they establish a harmonic relationship while retaining their linear individuality [音乐]对位
credential	n.	someone's education, achievements, experience, etc. that prove they have the ability to do something 某人可以得到信任的证明

D

décor	n.	the style in which the inside of a building is decorated 装饰布局/风格
default	n.	failure to perform a task or fulfill an obligation, especially failure to meet a financial obligation 未履行债务，拖欠
detoxify	v.	to remove harmful substances or poisons from sth 解毒，祛毒
dire	adj.	disastrous, urgent, or terrible 危难的，急迫的
disenfranchised	adj.	deprived of the rights of citizenship especially the right to vote 被剥夺了公民权利的
distill	v.	to separate or extract the essential elements of 提炼
dividend	n.	a part of a company's profit that is divided among the people with shares in the company 红利
drudgery	n.	hard boring work 苦活，单调乏味的工作

E

emulate	v.	to strive to equal or excel, especially through imitation 模仿，仿照
enclave	n.	a small area that is within a larger area where people of a different kind or nationality live 飞地（被外国领地包围的土地）
euphoria	n.	a feeling of great happiness or well-being 幸福感
Euro	n.	Euro (Football) Cup 200X 欧洲杯
exotic	adj.	from another part of the world; foreign 异国的
expel	v.	to officially force someone to leave a school or organization 驱逐，开除

F

fake fouls	v. phr.	Pretend to foul 假犯规

felony	n.	an offense, as murder or burglary, of graver character than those called misdemeanors 重罪
flaunt	v.	to show your money, success, beauty, etc. so that other people notice it — used to show disapproval 炫耀，夸耀
formidable	adj.	very powerful or impressive, and often frightening 强大的
franchise	n.	a permission given by a company to someone who wants to sell its goods or services 特许权
fusion	n.	sth new created by a mixture of qualities, ideas, or things 融合

G

gain traction	v. phr.	making progress 取得进展
garner	v.	to acquire or to deserve by one's efforts or actions 获得
geezer	n.	(*BrE*) a man 人
GI	n.	a soldier in the US army, especially during the Second World War 美国大兵
gorgeous	adj.	splendid or sumptuous in appearance, coloring, etc.; magnificent 恢宏的
grandeur	n.	impressive beauty, power, or size 宏伟，壮观
griot	n.	a storyteller in western Africa who perpetuates the oral tradition and history of a village or family 讲故事的人
gripe	n.	sth unimportant that you complain about 抱怨，牢骚
groom	v.	to take care of your own appearance by keeping your hair and clothes clean and tidy 修饰个人外貌和衣着
grumble	n.	complaint 抱怨，埋怨

H

harry	v.	to keep asking someone for something in a way that is upsetting or annoying 折磨
Hispanics	n.	a Spanish-speaking person; a U.S. citizen or resident of Latin-American or Spanish descent 讲西班牙语的人，拉美裔或西班牙裔美国公民
hop	v.	to get on a plane, bus, train, etc., especially after suddenly deciding to do so 乘飞机飞越，跳上（火车、飞机、汽车等）
hype	n.	attempts to make people think something is good or important by talking about it a lot on television, the radio, etc., used to show disapproval 炒作

I

iconoclastic	adj.	attacking and seeking to overthrow traditional or popular ideas or institutions 抨击并试图推翻传统、流行的思想或制度

imposing	adj.	impressive, magnificent 令人印象深刻的
in a different light	prep. phr.	If someone or something is seen or shown in a particular light, people can see that particular part of their character 刮目相看
inaccessible	adj.	impossible or very difficult to reach 很难达到的，难以接近的
incrementally	adv.	of, relating to, being, or occurring in especially small increments as "incremental additions" or "incremental change" 逐步增加
intercede	v.	to act as mediator in a dispute 调解
interlude	n.	a short piece of music, talk, etc. used to fill a short period of time between the parts of a play, concert, etc. 间奏曲
intractable	adj.	difficult, troublesome 困难的，棘手的
intrinsic	adj.	of or relating to the essential nature of a thing; inherent 内在的

J

jerky	adj.	foolish, silly 傻里傻气的

K

kick-start	v.	to do sth to help a process or activity start or develop more quickly 使启动
kinky	adj.	having or showing unusual ways of getting sexual excitement 怪异的
knockout	n.	a competition in which competitors are eliminated progressively 淘汰赛
knot	n.	a small group of people standing close together 群，簇

L

limelight	n.	a focus of public attention 公众注意
lochs	n.	a lake or a part of the sea partly enclosed by land in Scotland（苏格兰）湖，狭长的海湾
lure	v.	to attract by wiles or temptation; entice 引诱

M

make a dent	v. phr.	an appreciable consequence (especially a lessening)

			影响，结果
makeshift		adj.	improvised, temporary 临时的
mania		n.	a strong desire for something or interest in something, especially one that affects a lot of people at the same time; craze 狂
mantra		n.	a word or sound that is repeated as a prayer or to help people meditate（宗）颂歌
matey		adj.	(Br infml) friendly or intimate 亲密的
maven		n.	(AmE) someone who knows a lot about a particular subject 行家
mesh		n.	to fit together closely or work in harmony 配合密切，工作协调
minder		n.	someone who is employed to protect another person 看管者
miscall		v.	to call by a wrong name 点错名字，张冠李戴
miscegenation		n.	the interbreeding of different races or of persons of different racial backgrounds 异族通婚
moratorium		n.	an official stopping of an activity for a period of time 暂停，终止
mutate		n.	an alteration or change, as in nature, form, or quality 演变

N

netball		n.	Netball is a non-contact generally indoor sport similar to, and derived from, basketball. It is usually known as a women's sport. It was originally known in its country of origin, the United States, as "women's basketball". 是类似篮球的女子运动，最早的名字是叫"女子篮球"，起源于美国，创始人：Clara Gregory Baer, 中文翻译有好几个，有"篮网球"，"投球"，"英式女篮"，没有统一的中文名字。风行於美、英、加、澳、纽、斯里兰加及西印度群岛。即"无挡板篮球"或"女子篮球"。
newfangled		adj.	recently designed or produced usually used to show disapproval or distrust 新玩艺儿的
niche		n.	an opportunity to sell a product or service to a particular group of people who have similar needs, interests, etc. 针对具有类似需求或兴趣的产品或服务
no-holds-barred		adj.	(only before noun) a no-holds-barred discussion, situation, etc. is one in which there are no rules or limits 无限制的
noxious		adj.	harmful, poisonous 有害的，有毒的
nuptials		n. pl.	a wedding 婚礼

O

oasis		n.	an area in the desert where there is water and where plants grow 绿洲

oblivion	n.	the condition or quality of being completely forgotten 彻底忘记
Oedipal	adj.	related to an Oedipus complex恋母情结的，（希腊神话）俄狄浦斯的
off kilter	prep. phr.	sth just not right; off balance 不太对劲
organic	adj.	happening in a natural way, without anyone planning it or forcing it to happen 自然的，纯朴的

P

panic	v.	to affect or be affected with panic 吓慌
paradigm	n.	(technical) a model or example that shows how something works or is produced 范式，模范
parka	n.	a thick warm jacket with a hood 带风帽的外套
pedagogy	n	the art or method of teaching; pedagogics 教学，教学法
permafrost	n.	a layer of soil that is always frozen in countries where it is very cold 永冻层
pi	n.	an orchestra pit 乐池
pitch	n.	A "football pitch" is the playing surface for the game of association football made of turf. Its dimensions and markings are defined by Law 1 of the Laws of the Game, "The Field of Play". 球场
plight	n.	a situation from which extrication is difficult especially an unpleasant or trying one 窘况
polemic	n.	a controversial argument, especially one refuting or attacking a specific opinion or doctrine 辩论
pollster	n.	someone who works for a company that prepares and asks questions to find out what people think about a particular subject 民意调查者
posh	adj.	smart and fashionable 时尚的
posse	n.	(slang) a group of friends or associates 一帮
premiered	adj.	to present the first public performance of 首演的
pro	n.	a professional, especially in sports 职业（球员等）
proactive	adj.	making things happen or change rather than reacting to events 积极主动的
prod	v.	to goad to action; incite.
prohibitively	adv.	prohibiting, forbidding 禁止的
propel	v.	to cause to move forward or onward 推动
proprietary	adj.	being used, produced, or marketed under exclusive legal right of the inventor or maker; specifically: a drug (as a patent medicine) that is protected by secrecy, patent, or copyright

		against free competition as to name, product, composition, or process of manufacture 受专利保护的
prospective	adj.	likely to become or be 可能成为的
pummel	v.	to beat repeatedly as with the fists 砸
pump iron	v. phr.	(infml) weight lifting 举重

R

rabid	adj.	extremely zealous or enthusiastic; fanatical 狂热的
ramshackle	adj.	tumbledown, dilapidated, broken down 坍塌的
ravishingly	adv.	extremely attractive; entrancing 十分迷人地，令人倾倒地
reconfigure	v.	to rearrange the elements or settings of 重新安排，重新规划
refurbish	v.	to renovate and brighten up 装修，翻新
repertory	n.	a type of theatre work in which actors perform different plays on different days 不同时间的演出剧目
rev up	v.	speed up 加速
rever	v.	to regard with awe, deference, and devotion 敬畏
roiling	adj.	(of a liquid) agitated vigorously; turbulent 搅浑的
rustic	adj.	simple, old-fashioned, and not spoiled by modern developments, in a way that is typical of the countryside 乡村的

S

sabra	n.	(esp US) Israeli Jew bon in Israel 土生土长的以色列人
salivate	v.	(infml) to be full of desire or eagerness for sth 垂涎，流口水
sample	v.	to try an activity, go to a place, etc. in order to see what it is like 尝试
sanatorium	n.	a place like a hospital where patients who have a lasting illness or who are getting better after an illness are treated 疗养院，休养所
savor	v.	to fully enjoy a time or experience 欣赏，品味
sceptic	n.	someone who habitually doubts accepted beliefs 怀疑一切的人
Schizophrenic	n.	someone who has a serious mental illness in which his thoughts and feelings are not based on what is really happening around him 精神分裂症患者
scuffle	v.	to fight, come to blows 打架
seamlessly	adv.	Done or made so smoothly that you cannot tell where one thing stops and another begins 连贯地
septet	n.	a composition for seven voices or seven instruments 七重奏
shaman	n.	a person in some religions and societies who is believed to be able to contact good and evil spirits and cure people of illnesses 萨满

shin	n.	the front part of your leg between your knee and your foot 胫部
sinuous	adj.	lithe, twisting 弯的，蜿蜒曲折的
sizzling	adj.	(esp AmE) very hot 很热的
slate	v.	If something is slated to happen, it is planned to happen in the future, especially at a particular time 规划，（按照目前的形势发展）一定要发生
sluggish	adj.	moving or reacting more slowly than normal 慢吞吞的
sneer	v.	to smile or speak in a very unkind way that shows you have no respect for someone or something 讥讽
sophistication	n.	the process or result of becoming more complex, developed, or subtle 精湛程度
speckle	v.	to cover with small marks or spots 带有斑点
sprawl	n.	a large area covered with buildings that spreads from the city into the countryside in an ugly way (城市)杂乱无序拓展的地区
squad	n.	a group of players from which a team will be chosen for a particular sports event 小组，小队
squeamish	adj.	excessively fastidious or scrupulous 过于挑剔，指责的
staggering	adj.	causing great astonishment, amazement, or dismay; overwhelming 令人瞠目结舌的
stereotype	n.	a belief or idea of what a particular type of person or thing is like, often unfair or untrue 成见
stranded	adj.	a person or vehicle that is stranded is unable to move from the place where they are 搁浅的，被困的，未得到帮助的
surcharge	n.	an additional sum added to the usual amount or cost 附加费

T

taboo	n.	a social or religious custom prohibiting or restricting a particular practice or forbidding association with a particular person, place, or thing 禁忌
taint	v.	to stain, pollute 弄污，玷污
thoroughfare	n.	the main road through a place such as a city or village 主要大街，通衢
thrift	n.	frugality 勤俭
to be dismissive of	phr.	refusing to consider someone or something seriously 不屑一顾
tony	adj.	marked by an elegant or exclusive manner or quality 精品的，高档次的
trade-off	n.	a balance between two opposing things, that you are willing to accept in order to achieve something 权衡，协调

trek	n.	a long, hard walk lasting several days or weeks, especially in the mountains 长途跋涉，艰难的旅程
trigonometry	n.	the part of mathematics concerned with the relationship between the angles and sides of triangles 三角学
troupe	n.	a group of singers, actors, dancers, etc. who work together 剧团
turbulent	adj.	disorderly 杂乱无章的
turn-out	n.	(*singular*) the number of people who go to a party, meeting, or other organized event 聚集的人群

U

ubiquitous	adj.	ever-present, everywhere 到处可见的
underscore	v.	highlight, emphasize 强调
unstructured	adj.	not organized in a detailed way, and allowing people freedom to do what they want 松散的，自由的
upside	n.	an advantageous aspect 有利的方面
usurp	v.	seize, grab 夺取，篡权

V

vest	v.	become legally vested
viable	adj.	capable of success or continuing effectiveness; practicable 可行的
virtuosity	n.	intelligence, genius 聪明，天才
vitality	n.	vivacity, liveliness, vigor 活力
void	n.	a situation in which sth important or interesting is needed or wanted, but does not exist 空白
voilà	interj.	(*French*) used when you are showing or telling someone something surprising 瞧（表示惊讶或满意之感叹词）

W

whisk	v.	to move or cause to move with quick light sweeping motions 急速（驶去）
wrench	n.	a metal tool that you use for turning nuts 扳手
write-off	n.	an official agreement that someone does not have to pay a debt 免除债务的声明

Z

zip	v.	to go somewhere or do something very quickly 急匆匆地做